LUKE'S MESSA

GOOD NE
FOR THE NEW MILLENNIUM

J. ELLSWORTH KALAS

Abingdon Press
Nashville

Luke's Message: Good News for the New Millennium
by J. Ellsworth Kalas

Scripture quotations in this publication, unless otherwise indicated, are
from the New Revised Standard Version of the Bible, copyrighted ©
1989 by the Division of Christian Education of the National Council of
the Churches of Christ in the United States of America, and are used
by permission. All rights reserved.

ISBN 0-687-05654-3

This book is printed on acid-free paper.

Manufactured in the United States of America.

03 04 05 06 — 10 9 8

TABLE OF CONTENTS

Meet the Writer

A native of Sioux City, Iowa, J. Ellsworth Kalas received his bachelor's degree from the University of Wisconsin (1951) with a variety of honors and his Master of Divinity degree from Garrett-Evangelical Theological Seminary (1954) with distinction. He has received honorary doctorates from Lawrence University (1965) and Asbury Theological Seminary (1986).

Dr. Kalas served thirty-eight years as a parish pastor. The first twenty-two years were in Wisconsin, the next sixteen at the Church of the Savior (United Methodist) in Cleveland, Ohio.

In July, 1988, Dr. Kalas became the associate in evangelism with the World Methodist Council, with an emphasis on spiritual renewal in local congregations and special programs for the clergy.

On July 1, 1993, Dr. Kalas became the first Beeson Senior Pastor in Residence at the new Beeson School of Preaching at Asbury Theological Seminary, Wilmore, Kentucky. In this role he serves as teacher and mentor to the Beeson Scholars and as adjunct professor in the D.Min. program.

A Word of Welcome

Welcome to LUKE'S MESSAGE: GOOD NEWS FOR THE NEW MILLENNIUM. We hope you enjoy this fresh new look at the Gospel of Luke. This six-session study will enrich your understanding of this Gospel and will provide a worthy pursuit of the gospel truth as we approach the third millennium.

This study is thematic; it does not begin with the first chapter of Luke and proceed through reports of Jesus' ministry to the Resurrection. Rather, the study is organized around six life-oriented questions to help you examine in a renewed way the life and teachings of Jesus.

The Six Questions

As we approach the new millennium, many of us have turned our minds to what the new century will bring, and what it means for us. The sessions in this study help us with that reflection. Listed at the top of the next column are the questions around which the sessions are organized:

What was Luke's world like?
What was Luke's Gospel about?
What does Luke teach us about the human condition?
What does Luke teach us about Jesus Christ?
How does Luke teach us to understand our lives?
What does Luke teach us about living in the third millennium?

Within each lesson there are ample references to the Scriptures that illumine the responses to the question. When possible, we have tried to let Luke speak to us afresh today.

Studying Luke Successfully

LUKE'S MESSAGE can be used successfully as a self-study or as a group study. Reflection and discussion questions are in boxes at the bottom of the pages throughout the book. The questions refer to information on that page or on an adjacent page.

Use these questions for quiet reflection or as conversation starters. Some of them ask for data: When did something happen? What did Jesus say or do about an event or experience? Others ask for more evaluative responses: Why, do you think, did Jesus treat someone in a particular way? Still other questions personalize the Gospel: What does this ancient teaching mean for you or for the church today?

In each instance, the text will draw you closer into Luke's world and help you bridge the centuries from the time when Jesus lived and taught to your time, when Jesus' teaching remains alive and vibrant for today.

Reflection Partners

If you are studying Luke in a group or on your own, you may want a reflection or prayer partner to talk to and pray with during the time between the study sessions. There are more than enough discussion starters to sustain a class; you have more questions to pique your interest than you can cover. You may enjoy pursuing the questions on your own or praying with a partner about the concerns that arise during the study time.

Making a Commitment

You may find during or at the end of your study that you are ready to affirm or reaffirm a commitment of your life to Jesus Christ. We encourage you to reflect carefully on the message Jesus Christ brings to you through the words of Luke. Do they engage you to grow into a deeper, more complete relationship with God? Do they bring new light to biblical passages that had been unclear or a stumbling block to real understanding?

If you are inspired to a new level of commitment, discuss it with your pastor, your study leader, or a committed friend in the faith. You will find support and welcome. Remember, you

1

LUKE'S WORLD

9/12

We cannot help reading the Bible in a somewhat self-centered way. We have been told that the Bible will speak to our needs, and many of us have found that it does; so we pick it up with that expectation. That means that we do a kind of immediate translation; we take a book—like Luke—from the first century A.D. and read it as if it belonged to this time between the twentieth and twenty-first centuries. And of course, in one sense it does, because the message of the Bible is timeless.

The Book of Luke

But the books of the Bible come from particular times and cultures, with the distinct nuances of different languages. Because this is so, we do well now and then to examine the womb from which the books were born. We will understand them better and appreciate them more if we do. And the sooner in our study that we do so, the better we will grasp all that follows.

The book is Luke, and we ask ourselves about the world in which Luke was written. When we ask about Luke's world, we naturally mean—whether we say it or not—Luke's world in comparison to our own.

We assume that Luke's world was vastly different. By some measures we are right in this assumption. Luke's world had no jet planes, no computers or fax machines, no television or miracle drugs. Most of the items on our restaurant menus would be incomprehensible in Luke's world.

This very standard of comparison says a great deal about us. It

What are some of the ways in which life in Luke's day is different from our own? is similar to our own? Is this comparison valuable to you in any way? If so, how?

suggests that we think the most significant issues of life are physical, mechanical, and electronic. And of course they matter, because they are the context in which we live. But so many crucial factors of life are the same in our time as they were in A.D. 60. People then ate, drank, worked, conceived children, and died, as they do now. They experienced joy, fear, ambition, aspiration, and dread, just as we do.

Still and all, we are in many ways shaped and made different by our environment. A world of traffic lights is in a pragmatic way more regimented than a world where courtesy determined whose ox went first at a crossroads. We sometimes are astonished by the differences in lifestyle that we experience when we go from a great urban center in a particular country to a bucolic rural area. How much more, then, if we go from the twentieth and twenty-first centuries to the first century.

Luke: A Product of Ethnic Influences

Luke's days were lived out at an intersection of three powerful ethnic influences. Politically, there was Rome. No kingdom before it had been so widespread and so efficiently organized, and probably not many since could compete with it for sheer administrative excellence. We think of the Romans today for the roads they left behind, some of which are still modest marvels of engineering. Those roads were only an iceberg tip of the strength Rome brought to the first-century world. With an empire stretching from Britain to Mesopotamia, with all of North Africa including Egypt, Rome was able to enforce a structure of peace for some two hundred years, the almost legendary Pax Romana. This factor of world peace provided possibilities for world commerce that had only been a dream before. Needless to say, it also was crucial to the early spread of the

What Roman accomplishments (of all kinds) aided in the spread of Christianity?

What impact might you imagine the Pax Romana had on the survival of Christianity? What factors aid in its spread today?

The Jews and new Christians brought a high ethical quality to life among Greek and Roman society. What qualities of religious belief and practice set us apart from our society today? integrate us in our society?

gospel. Paul and the other early Christian missionaries could travel over the entire Empire on good roads and bridges and with relative safety, never having to worry about war or competing governments.

Culturally, Greece was the dominant influence, as it had been for several centuries before Luke's time. At the height of their greatness, the Greeks had developed ideas of democracy and human rights that are still influential today, and their city-states were for a time legendary. But by the time of Luke, Greece had long ceased to be a political or military influence. Culturally, however, it became a greater influence than ever, because the Romans spread the art, philosophy, and lifestyle of Greece throughout the vast Roman Empire.

And what was especially important, the Romans spread the Greek language. It is said that one could travel anywhere in the vast Mediterranean world in the first century and communicate easily if only one knew Greek. There could never have been a better time for a message to be set loose in the world, because wherever one went, the message could be communicated and understood.

> **A world of traffic lights is in a pragmatic way more regimented than a world where courtesy determined whose ox went first at a crossroads.**

Luke himself was probably a Greek, and his Gospel shows it in any number of positive ways.

Religiously, the Jews were a power to be reckoned with. In spiritual matters, they were significant out of all proportion to their size. Other peoples often despised them, yet were influenced by them. In a world where gods were available on every corner, the Jews dared to say that there was only one God. By their doing so, they were seen by many as atheists, because to believe in only one god seemed to be a denial of god. The Jews insisted that religion must include an ethical quality, a quite indifferent issue for the vast number of first-century religionists who cherished religion for its presumed powers of magic.

One should not overestimate the general influence of the Jews upon first-century religion, but of course their influence on Luke was profound. No one could travel with Paul, as Luke did, and not feel the impact of Judaism on religious thought. Paul was often despised by his former associates in the Jewish faith, and he might often seem to have been dramatically at odds with them. Nevertheless, he was a product of Judaism and drew his hopes from the best expectations of that faith; and Luke, as his beloved physician and associate, partook of Paul's heritage.

Education in Luke's World

We are likely to look upon the first century, so far removed in time from our own, as quite primitive. In truth, the first century was a time of particularly widespread literacy. Some scholars feel, in fact, that it was the period of widest literacy for fully eighteen centuries to come.

In Palestine, for example, nearly every village had its own school, with compulsory education for everyone over the age of six. Perhaps the most powerful element in the Jewish attitude toward education was its link to their religious faith. It is not incidental that they perceived that the Law had come to them in writing, which of itself placed an obligation upon them to be a learned people, so they could read the commandments of God. The Wisdom Literature of the Hebrew Scriptures exalted the importance of being an educated people and of maintaining a lifelong pursuit of wisdom. Young Jewish children selected their own personal text from the Scriptures that contained the same letters as their Hebrew name. This reinforced a kind of mystical attitude toward learning, raising it far above a mere compiling of knowledge.

Education was not as universal in the Greek and Roman world, and its goals were different. Education was largely the realm of males, although Roman girls received at least a rudimentary education. The teaching tended to emphasize what we today would call a classical education, with literature, music, rhetoric, philosophy, and mathematics leading the way, but with some systems also giving a large place to medicine, architecture, astronomy, drawing,

---

What were some of the educational practices of the ancient world?

For Jews and early Christians, education was religious education. What impact did that orientation to learning have on new Christians? What attitude do churches have today about learning and about the value of religious education?

The Jews believed that their Law came to them in writing. How well have our churches united "knowledge and vital piety"? How does your congregation value the formational and transformational aspects of biblical learning?

optics, and history. Roman education was more practically oriented than the Greek system.

All of this means that Luke wrote his books for an age that prized knowledge and in which the ability to read was more nearly universal than in our relatively modern period. The production of books was of course laborious, so individual copies of manuscripts were hard to come by. But this may only have meant that people sought the more earnestly to get what was available and that they sought out the discussions that their reading evoked. In any event, learning was prized.

In a sense, we have firsthand evidence in Luke's prologue to his Gospel, when he tells us that "many have undertaken to set down an orderly account of the events" of Jesus' life (Luke 1:1). How remarkable that within a few years after Jesus' brief ministry, death, and resurrection, "many" should have bothered to write biographies and records of various lengths. This reflects both their love for Christ and the "market" for what they were writing. Luke lived in an intellectually hungry age where, in spite of obstacles, people sought the chance to read and to learn.

> **Luke lived in an intellectually hungry age where, in spite of obstacles, people sought the chance to read and to learn.**

Social Structures in Luke's World

We must be careful when we discuss the social structures of another day lest we read history as if it were a checkout-counter tabloid. Every generation has its horror stories, and it is important to keep such matters in perspective. If we are dealing with statistics, we want to be sure that our source is dependable. If our data is anecdotal, we need to know if it is typical of the times, or whether it is remembered simply because it is out of the ordinary.

With those reservations in mind, let us acknowledge that the first-century world was quite different from ours in several ways. Society was much more stratified, with little opportunity for a person to move from one level to another. The role of women was severely restricted. Divorce in most first-century cultures was essentially impossible for a woman, but available almost at will for a man. In proper Greek society, a respectable woman was rarely seen in public life; she was never seen on the streets alone. The man, meanwhile, enjoyed freedom that could easily be profligate. Mind you, that depended on the character of the man; but from a human point of view, when the boundaries of life are broadly extended, even a careful person will take liberties he or she might not otherwise take.

But if anything defined with special clarity the tragic aspects of first-century sociological life, it would be the prevalence of slavery. Students of social structures say that slavery is almost as old as the agricultural economy and certainly as old as war—the easiest method of getting slaves. But slavery may have reached its peak in the first century. The Greek civilization of the third and fourth centuries B.C. was built on the existence of a slave class. It is responsibly said that slaves constituted as much as one third of the population in many cities in the first century. Slavery was, in fact, so commonplace and so taken-for-granted that it was seen as a natural way of life. Probably many slaves had the same estimate of themselves.

Morally, perhaps the worst thing about slavery is that it caused a great body of people to be seen as less-than-human. The slaves who worked in mines and in other hazardous occupations were treated as poorly as any animal. On the other hand, some trusted household slaves were allowed to eat with the family to whom they belonged, and many were teachers or physicians. Nevertheless, they were still slaves and were not free to choose their own way of life, except in those instances where they were able to gain their freedom.

Such was Luke's world. It was brilliant with love of learning and art, and with widespread education, but with moral structures that worried little about the helpless and the disadvantaged and that assumed that it was proper and normal for one human being to own another. And it was a world where gods were so plentiful that in Athens an altar was erected to "an unknown god," just

What was the role of women in the ancient social structures of Luke's era? the role of slavery?

How does one's place within the social/economic structure influence one's access to the good news? What impact does that place have on how the gospel message is understood?

What special message does Luke's Gospel carry for persons who are helpless and disadvantaged? What do those of power and advantage need to hear from the Gospel?

How might Luke help us define loyalty in the faith? in the Christian community?

in case one had been missed (Acts 17:23). But it was also, for all of these reasons both negative and positive, a world dramatically in need of a saving message. It was to this world that Luke addressed his good news.

Who Was Luke?

So who was Luke, whose name is attached to this book? Although, unlike the other Gospel writers, he uses the first person singular in the prologue to his book, Luke never names himself. It is others who identify him as the author of this Gospel. As a matter of fact, the authorities whose opinion we usually seek, the Christian writers from the first several centuries, are unanimous in doing so. The Muratorian Canon (late second century A.D.) and Irenaeus (ca. 130–200), the first great Christian theologian, both identify the author of this Gospel as the Luke who traveled with Paul. Many early writers considered him to be the anonymous second party (with Cleopas) in the Emmaus Road resurrection appearance by Jesus (Luke 24). If that be so, Luke was one of the first to see the resurrected Lord, and the Emmaus story would have the special quality of a firsthand account.

Jerome (ca. 345–420), who gave us the Vulgate version of the

Perhaps Luke's extraordinary empathy for the disadvantaged sprang from some personal experiences as an outsider.

Bible, puts his feelings into less scholarly, more graphic, language: "Luke the physician, by leaving us his Gospel and his Acts of the Apostles has shown us how the Apostles became from fishers of fish fishers of men; for he himself became from a physician of the body a physician of the soul." And then, in a lovely touch, Jerome says: "As often as his book is read in the Church, so often does his medicine flow out."

Modern scholarship usually produces several theories about the authorship of any biblical book, because there are so many ways of marshaling evidence and interpreting data. But certainly no Gospel is more substantially supported in its authorship than is Luke. It is not only that the earliest Christian writers so surely take him for granted, but also that he would hardly have been selected if the evidence were not so strong. For one thing, he was a kind of outsider, since he is the only non-Jew among the New Testament writers. Also, he is a relatively obscure personality in the New Testament; if the early church were looking for a personality who would add stature to a book, they would not have chosen Luke.

But what kind of person was

he? As we have already seen, in the quotation from Jerome, Luke was a physician. Paul so identifies him in the Letter to the Colossians: "Luke, the beloved physician" (Colossians 4:14)—or "the dear doctor," as someone has put it. Because he traveled with Paul, it is generally concluded that he served as Paul's personal physician; Paul probably needed such, because he hints of a variety of afflictions, yet maintains the kind of rigorous schedule that would be calculated to aggravate those afflictions.

Our first inclination, when we think of Luke as a physician, may be to imagine him just a step or two above a purveyor of magic, or at best, to sentimentalize him as a loving though ill-trained man. We need to remind ourselves that it was some four hundred years earlier that Hippocrates had raised medicine to the level of a science and had left us with what is still the classic definition of medical ethics. And for that matter, it was in the generation after Luke that the Greek physician, Galen, who practiced in Rome, introduced the field of experimental medicine through his work with ani-mals. But Luke's own Gospel makes a point, in that it uses terminology that is suggestive of the medical profession in his day. It was, indeed, a learned field; by no means as sophisticated as it is in our day, but on the other hand, not too far removed from the style of medicine our grandparents knew.

But as I indicated earlier, in the first-century world a substantial number of doctors were slaves. This probably indicates that they were physicians in their own country; and when they were captured in war, their new owners chose to put them to the same use. Some scholars feel that Luke's name, which is a contraction of some longer name, is one often attached to slaves. If slavery was part of Luke's heritage, he felt right at home in the early Christian church, where so many were slaves. And this may lend further insight to some of the qualities that are so evident in Luke's book. Perhaps his extraordinary empathy for the disadvantaged sprang from some personal experiences as an outsider.

We will notice, as we continue our study, that Luke seems to be a very sensitive man. Some connect

What do we know about Luke? What added information is provided by tradition?

What actions, attitudes, or characteristics do you admire about Luke? In what ways can you identify with him and his ministry?

What contribution does Luke make to the church today?

this quality with his being a physician; certainly we expect physicians, at their best, to be sensitive persons, and probably many people who pursue a career in medicine are first drawn to the field by their innate concern for humans and their pain. In any event, perhaps it is partly because of Luke's quality of sensitivity that an ancient tradition says that he was a painter, and a skilled one. Tradition dating back to the Middle Ages says that he did a portrait of Mary, the mother of Jesus, a picture that exists in a cathedral in Rome.

Naturally there is something very appealing about thinking that Luke might have painted a picture of the Virgin Mary, even though the odds against its continuing to our day seem very great. It is because of these several traditions that Luke has been the patron saint of painters since the fourteenth century.

The apostle Paul makes a passing reference to Luke that underlines something of the quality of his character. As the apostle draws near to the conclusion of the Second Letter to Timothy, he takes a somewhat sad tone, noting those who have left for one reason or another. And then he adds, "Only Luke is with me" (2 Timothy 4:11).

One should not put too many evidences of pathos into those

Even a superficial reading of this Gospel indicates that Luke had a heart for "the least, the last, and the lost."

few words, and yet it seems typical of Luke that he would remain by Paul's side after others were gone. For many centuries the church has symbolized the four Gospel writers with the figures envisioned by the prophet Ezekiel (Ezekiel 1:10) and the writer of Revelation (4:6b-10)—a human being, a lion, an ox, and an eagle. Perhaps it is the purest chance that Luke, being third among the Gospels, is thus identified with the ox; but it is also wonderfully appropriate because Luke seems by character to possess the servant, burden-bearing heart. But the winged quality of Ezekiel's vision also fits, because Luke is surely an ox that soars. His language, his insight, and his sense of divine grandeur insist that we rise up with him.

Speaking of Luke's language, let it be noted that he must have been a very learned man. His Greek in the opening paragraph is often compared favorably with classical Greek writers. It is also a book of rare beauty; some have even described it as the most beautiful book ever written. It is a rare writer indeed who can combine scholarly excellence with artistic loveliness.

But of course our best understanding of Luke, both as a person and as a follower of Christ, will come as we read his book. Authors almost inevitably reveal either what they are, or what they wish they were. The four Gospel writers are all dealing with essentially the same body of material, the events and teachings from the life of Jesus. Each writer selects the material that best fits his own personality and—especially—those elements in Jesus that he wants most to convey to his particular circle of readers.

So when we read Luke's Gospel we learn a great deal about Luke even as we learn about Jesus. It will be more than Luke, the scholar, or Luke, the historian; above all, it will be a picture of Luke, the believer, and especially Luke, the evangelist; a person who has been transformed by Jesus Christ and who wants passionately to offer that transformation to others. I come away from Luke's Gospel liking Luke a very great deal, and wishing I might have known him personally. He would, as they say, bear acquaintance.

To Whom Was Luke Writing?

While anyone may read any of the four Gospels with profit, we will also sense in our reading that each Gospel writer must have had a particular audience in mind. Popular tradition says that Matthew was aiming especially at the Jews, and there is easy evidence for such a conclusion. Mark seems to have had a Roman audience in mind, while John wrote to established believers who were ready to receive his profound convictions. And Luke was aiming, particularly, at the Greeks. For a student of the Greek language, this fact comes through in the language itself. On the one hand, as I mentioned earlier, his Greek is among the best in the New Testament, often marked by sheer elegance. Thus, Luke will take material that is also

What images, stories, terms, attitudes in the Gospel of Luke make it most accessible to you? What touches you personally? What confuses you? What helps make it your story?

What kinds of things will you be looking for as you read this Gospel? (For example: how Luke characterizes "people on the margins" or how his compassion for people influences the way Jesus is presented)

What does Luke teach about those who are most often overlooked? Review Luke 16:19-31, for example.

found in Mark's Gospel (that scholars assume is the earliest record) and will polish and refine it, much the way an accomplished editor would revise an earnest but unsophisticated manuscript. Greek is clearly more native to Luke than to Mark.

But on the other hand, Luke uses Semitic idioms as well. One senses a powerful ambivalence in what Luke is doing with language. He wants to place his message in the most powerful and eloquent vehicle at his disposal, and he has the power to do so, because he knows Greek so well. But he wants also to convey the nuances of life and meaning that are possible only in the language in which the message was originally spoken, Aramaic. So he slips in the figures of speech and the rhythms that would be native to that language. Very few of us are in a position fully to appreciate what Luke was trying to do, but we can still be properly in awe of his sense of mission and of the skill with which he fulfilled it.

It seems to me that Luke shows his sacred ambivalence in another way. Even a superficial reading of this Gospel indicates that Luke had a heart for "the least, the last, and the lost." It is he who gives us the parable of the prodigal and

Luke would be astonished, but perhaps not surprised; perhaps he knew that he was handling the elements of eternity.

who tells of Jesus' encounter with the despised tax collector, Zacchaeus—and gives us Jesus' gracious words to Zacchaeus and to the crowd that resented him: "For the Son of Man came to seek out and to save the lost" (Luke 19:10). It is Luke who so often tips his hand to the poor and to women, and who tells us the story of the rich man and Lazarus (Luke 16:19-31). Luke also tells us the delightful story of the Pharisee and the tax collector (Luke 18:9-14). All through his book, Luke pays particular and loving attention to those who are most easily overlooked.

And yet, as we have already noticed, his is the Gospel that must have been especially attractive to the learned and the cultured. No doubt he was a person who would have been at home in the academy. How remarkable that he chose to bridge these two very diverse worlds! It is the same quality that one finds in Florence Nightingale, who was born into a wealthy English home, but who chose to throw herself into what was at that time a despised occupation—nursing—and who in the end, lifted nursing to an esteemed profession. Or like Albert Schweitzer, one of the most able philosophical minds of the twentieth century, who chose to work among the people of Gabon, in tropical Africa.

So Luke seemed deliberately, perhaps rather effortlessly, to bridge the gap between the culture and learning so native to him and the rejected persons for whom he felt so much compassion. In this, he reflected the one who, though "in the form of God," abandoned his privileges and took "the form of a slave" (Philippians 2:6, 7).

What motivated Luke to reach out to his particular audience? Broadly speaking, he was doing what came naturally in his writing for a Greek audience, since he was himself Greek. It is more difficult to explain, however, why he seems to have aimed especially at disadvantaged elements of society. Perhaps, as we said earlier, he had served in slavery for a time, an experience that might have awakened empathy for others suffering human misfortune. Or perhaps there is no simple explanation, other than the sense of divine call that so often energizes people to give themselves inexplicably to particular persons and causes. Whatever the case, we modern readers are enriched by Luke's particular approach to the divine story.

In Summary

So here is Luke: a Greek among Jews, a scholar among sometimes pedestrian minds, a poet dealing with the common stuff of daily life. He lives in a time when slavery is commonplace and when social structures bring debasement to a sizable segment of the population. Nevertheless, it is a time of widespread learning and of very real cultural excitement. Luke decides he must tell that world, which already has a substantial number of accounts, his own orderly record of "the events that have been fulfilled among us" (Luke 1:1) and, later, continue the story of the followers of Jesus after the Master himself is gone.

And that world, against unbelievable odds, preserves what Luke has written, so that we read it today as we enter the third millennium. Luke would be astonished, but perhaps not surprised; perhaps he knew that he was handling the elements of eternity.

2

LUKE TELLS HIS STORY

Luke knows why he is writing his book, and he tells us why. His is not the first account of the life of Jesus; "many" have already done this project. We have no idea how many. Some scholars say that Luke wrote his Gospel as early as A.D. 60, while most others place it as late as the early 80's. In any event, Luke reasons that he ought to add to the collection that has already begun to accumulate by this time. He intends for his book to be "an orderly account." Luke is preparing it especially for the esteemed Theophilus (though he no doubt realizes that many others will see it—books were shared widely in those days, simply because of their scarcity), and he is anxious that the readers "may know the truth concerning the things about which [they] have been instructed" (Luke 1:4).

These are worthy aims, but of course they are only a small part of what must have been motivating Luke. As we see the things that Luke emphasizes, and the incidents he includes that the other Gospel writers have omitted, we realize that he had many reasons for writing his Gospel. It is not only that he wanted to give an orderly account, though his well-trained mind surely desired such an end, it is also that—being the kind of person he was—he could not resist including some poetry, some stories about women, and some dramatic evidence of Jesus' concern for the poorest and most despised of

Luke tells us that his aim is to give "an orderly account" of the story of Jesus (Luke 1:1-3). Is it fair to say that Luke has more in mind than simply to tell what other Gospel writers have also told?

What are the dates that scholars in general consider as the times when Luke might have written his Gospel? What date is suggested in your own study Bible?

the human race. Luke is a special kind of person, so he tells a special kind of story.

When Is the Beginning?

Matthew begins his account of the life of Jesus by giving us a genealogy. Mark begins with Jesus at age thirty, ready to embark on his mission, and John begins before the foundation of the earth, with Jesus as a partner in Creation. The beginning point depends on the story you want to tell. Luke begins with the kind of background information that newspaper writers might call a human interest story.

All of the Gospel writers tell us about John the Baptist. After all, he is the one who introduces Jesus' ministry. But Luke tells us the story behind John the Baptist's story. It is the wonderfully human story of a good husband and wife,

Zechariah and Elizabeth, who are "getting on in years," apparently well past the normal age of child-bearing and who have never been blessed with children (1:5-7). As Zechariah goes about his priestly duties in the sanctuary, he is confronted by an angel who announces that Zechariah and his wife will have a son and that the son shall be called John. This is indeed a special child, because "even before his birth he will be filled with the Holy Spirit" (1:16). Yes, and more; he will minister "with the spirit and power of Elijah" (1:17). Zechariah must have heard these words with special sensitivity, because it was commonly believed among the Jews that the coming of the Messiah would be preceded by a visit from the prophet Elijah.

Zechariah is a good man, but very human. He reminds the angel that he is "an old man" and

The four Gospels start in quite different ways, probably partly because they were aiming at different reading audiences. If you were going to write a Gospel today, how might you begin it for the community of faith? for a highly secular group?

As you consider the information Luke gives us in the stories of Zechariah and Elizabeth, and of the meeting between Elizabeth and Mary, what kind of person do you perceive Luke to be?

Look at the passages that refer to the Holy Spirit (Luke 1:15, 17, 41; 4:14). How would you interpret the work of the Spirit then? now?

Look also at some of the responses to the Holy Spirit (Luke 1:46, 48; 2:14, 29). How did those persons respond? How would you respond?

that his wife is "getting on in years"; so, appealing as the angel's promise might be, it is also unlikely. And for that, Zechariah is left mute until the child is born.

But Elizabeth conceives, as promised. In the sixth month of her pregnancy she is visited by a relative, Mary. Mary has just been visited by an angel, who has advised her that she will have a baby by the power of the Holy Spirit. Now Mary comes to her older relative to seek strength in her extraordinary assignment and is reaffirmed in dramatic fashion. When Elizabeth hears Mary's greeting, her own baby "leaped in her womb. And Elizabeth was filled with the Holy Spirit" (1:41). So Mary and Elizabeth enter into conversation and worship of God that would be possible only to two women who are at that moment pregnant, and who are uniquely chosen by God.

So it is that Luke begins his story: unhurried, with background information that is interesting in its own right and that will prove significant to the plot as the story unfolds. When Luke tells us that he is going to give an orderly account, we need to remember that each of us has his or her own definition of *orderly*. That is, we

> **Mary comes to her older relative to seek strength in her extraordinary assignment and is reaffirmed in dramatic fashion.**

are orderly to our own ends.

Luke is not orderly in the fashion of Matthew nor of Mark. Luke has an order that was pressed upon him by the Holy Spirit, and he is anxious to give it to us.

A major element in Luke's order is poetry. When Mary's calling is confirmed by her cousin Elizabeth, she breaks into song; we call it the *Magnificat*. When Zechariah's tongue is released after the naming of John, Zechariah also breaks into song. Mary had said, "My soul magnifies the Lord"; now Zechariah says, "Blessed be the Lord God of Israel" (1:46, 68). When "a multitude of the heavenly host" joins the angel who has told the shepherds that a Savior has been born, they do so with a song: "Glory to God in the highest heaven" (2:14); and we have the *Gloria*. When Joseph and Mary bring Jesus to the Temple for his presentation, the aged Simeon becomes a poet, with what centuries have called the *Nunc Dimittis*: "Master, now you are dismissing your servant in peace" (2:29).

So the baby is born, the angels sing, and the shepherds visit the manger, then return to their work, "glorifying and praising God" (2:20). Luke goes on to tell us of

Jesus' circumcision, of his presentation in the Temple, and of the exceeding joy that Anna and Simeon feel. But he tells us nothing of the wise men, nor of the flight to Egypt. He is working with a different order: "When they had finished everything required by the law of the Lord [that is, circumcision and presentation], they returned to Galilee, to their own town of Nazareth" (2:39).

And then Luke gives us one more human interest item. Alone among the Gospel writers, Luke tells us an incident from Jesus' boyhood. This is our only glimpse into the thirty years between Jesus' birth and the beginning of his public ministry. After this one brief vignette, Jesus returns to obscurity in Nazareth where he is obedient to his parents and where his mother "treasured all these things in her heart" (2:51). And Jesus grows up as any child might, increasing in "wisdom and in years [stature]," and also "in divine and human favor" (2:52). Luke has told us so little, and yet so much.

The Unfolding Ministry

Suddenly, it seems, Jesus is ready to leave the isolation of Nazareth and embark on his public ministry. Luke brings us to this point by recounting the phenomenon of John the Baptist's ministry— which, remarkable as it is, serves only as a prelude to John's baptism of Jesus. At this point Luke brings in, almost incidentally, what Matthew considers of primary importance, the genealogy of our Lord. But Luke uses different data than Matthew; and where Matthew begins in the past and works forward, Luke begins with Jesus and traces back, noting carefully that Jesus "was the son (as was thought) of Joseph" (Luke

What significance may be found in Luke's genealogy tracing back to Adam, rather than to Abraham?

We are sometimes inclined to think that Jesus' whole experience with temptation was in a brief period in the wilderness. What does the Scripture tell us about this experience (Luke 4:1-13)? Could it be that when Jesus was "praised by everyone" (4:15), this also was a temptation? Explain.

Logically, the religious leaders should have been Jesus' strongest supporters. Why do you think they responded to him so negatively? Look over several of the Scriptures in "The Unfolding Ministry" that describe Jesus' ministry. What example do they provide us?

3:23). Luke takes the genealogy all the way back to Adam, thus involving Jesus in the whole human race. And this, of course, is appropriate to Luke's whole theme, as we shall note later.

Now the preliminaries are done, except for one crucial event. Jesus goes into the wilderness for forty days of testing by the devil (4:1-13). It is his ordination examination by an utterly hostile interrogator. We are told only the concluding questions, the ones directed at him when he is at a natural point of hunger and exhaustion; of all that led up to these three questions we know nothing. Nor do we know the temptations that followed during the next three years; we only know that when this special temptation was past, the devil "departed from him until an opportune time" (4:13). I think the devil has many such times.

Now, full of the Spirit, Jesus returns to Galilee. He seems to have been an almost immediate sensation, "praised by everyone" (4:15). In the flush of this excitement he returns to Nazareth, where he had been brought up, and goes to the synagogue, "as was his custom," reads from the scroll and declares, "Today this scripture [Isaiah 61:1-2] has been fulfilled in your hearing" (4:21). At first the people respond with glad amazement, but then questions arise. Jesus meets the questions with challenges, and the people are "filled with rage" (4:28). Jesus' hometown will never again be the same.

As Jesus' reputation spreads, controversy comes with it. But his ministry in Galilee continues unabated.

Our Lord's continuing ministry in Galilee seems to unfold at a breakneck pace. Unclean spirits are cast out (4:31-37), persons are healed (4:38-41), disciples begin to be brought together (5:1-11), lepers are cleansed (5:12-16), a paralytic is healed (5:17-26), and even a tax collector joins Jesus' company (5:27-32). But of course we have no idea of the period of time in which these events unfolded. We sense that Jesus was on the road every day, healing, teaching, confronting adversaries both intellectual and spiritual.

As Jesus' reputation spreads, controversy comes with it. When Pharisees and teachers are present in what appears to have been an investigating delegation, Jesus seems intentionally to provoke them by forgiving a man's sins before healing him (5:17-26). He becomes still more incendiary when he prods the religious leaders on the crucial issue of the sabbath, first with a discussion (6:1-

5) and then with a healing (6:6-11). Already his enemies are "filled with fury" and wondering how they might dispose of Jesus.

But his ministry in Galilee continues unabated. There is teaching (just a small portion of Matthew's Sermon on the Mount), healing, and even a raising from the dead (7:11-17). Then the procession of excitement is interrupted by news from John the Baptist, and we realize how fragile are the elements that make up the Kingdom.

Next comes a magnificent incident, typical both of the kind of event Luke loved to report and of his style: the story of Jesus' dinner at the home of Simon the Pharisee (we are surprised that Jesus has been invited here), which is unceremoniously interrupted by "a woman . . . who was a sinner" (7:37). Luke conveys to us the compassion Jesus felt for an outsider (even allowing her to touch him was an act of mercy) and the artful way he took the curl of distaste from Simon's lip and forced

him to see the issues of God, sin, and forgiveness. To conclude, Jesus declared the woman forgiven and sent her on her way in peace. We sense, even as she leaves, that the others in the room remain unforgiven, because they cannot relate to mercy that extends beyond the boundaries of their kind.

It seems that Luke accelerates the pace in Chapters 8 and 9. We have a bit of teaching, the passing occasion with Jesus' mother and brothers, the calming of the storm, the healing of a demon-possessed man, the raising of Jairus's daughter, and the woman who got healing simply by touching Jesus' garment. Then, we read of the sending out of the Twelve, the feeding of the five thousand, Peter's declaration of faith, and the Transfiguration, with the healing that follows.

But "while everyone was amazed at all that he was doing" (9:43), Jesus burst the euphoria of the disciples by telling them that

Jesus told his disciples that he would soon be arrested, yet the disciples ignored this warning and discussed among themselves who would be greatest in the Kingdom they anticipated. How do you explain their insensitivity to Jesus' warning and their preoccupation with advancement?

Shortly after Jesus sets out to Jerusalem, we have the contrasting stories of would-be disciples who drop out and the commissioning and triumphant return of the seventy (Luke 9:57-62; 10:1-24). Why do you think Luke reports these two matters so close together?

LUKE'S MESSAGE

he was going to be handed over for arrest. The disciples didn't get it. Of course not, because they were so absorbed with arguments about who would be greatest when the Kingdom came that they could not grasp what kind of kingdom it was to be. With such self-absorption and insularity, they wanted to shut out any unapproved allies (9:49-50).

On to Jerusalem

Just here, Luke turns a corner. "When the days drew near for him to be taken up [to heaven], he set his face to go to Jerusalem" (9:51). All that happens for the rest of this Gospel until after the Resurrection occurs either on the way to Jerusalem or in that city.

Almost immediately Luke tells us a series of instances where would-be disciples drop by the wayside (9:57-62), then goes on to the commissioning of the seventy (or the seventy-two) and their early return in triumph (10:1-24). I sense a quality of impatience in this segment, as if Jesus were saying that the time is short, that there is no time for playing at religion.

In one brief encounter this mood of urgency takes a turn that seems unlikely for Luke's Gospel. Luke is especially solicitous of women, but when a woman in the crowd calls out a sweet and rather sentimental word, "Blessed is the womb that bore you and the breasts that nursed you!" Jesus' reply is almost sharp in its directness: "Blessed rather are those who hear the word of God and obey it!" (11:27-28). Sentiment has its place in life, and a very worthy place at that. But sometimes it must be pushed aside for the practical.

As Jesus heads to Jerusalem, sentiment is not enough; he is engaged to a cross. It is impossible—and for that matter, unnecessary—to make a detailed summary of the events and teachings as Jesus heads to Jerusalem. But let us look particularly at two matters, his parables and his particular encounters with people.

This section includes several parables that are familiar to us

Why would Jesus respond so abruptly to the woman who spoke to him with such sentimental warmth (Luke 11:27-28)? Can you think of some comparable instance in your own experience where someone responded to sentiment in such fashion? Is that kind of response ever justified?

Name some parables that we might call "parables of urgency." What do those parables say to you?

from Matthew and Mark, such as the mustard seed and the yeast (13:18-21), the great dinner and the lame excuses (14:15-24), the lost sheep (15:3-7), and the parable of the pounds or talents (19:11-27). Both Matthew and Luke place the parables of the dinner and the talents as the story mounts to its climax. It is easy to believe that Jesus told them at just such a time. Both parables have an air of urgency. It seems reasonable that Jesus may have spoken some of his parables numbers of times to different gatherings, the way a contemporary preacher or teacher will repeat material of presumed merit.

A majority of the longer parables in this section, however, are ones reported only by Luke. There are the two parables on prayer (11:5-8; 18:1-8). Both teach that prayer should be insistent and sustained. They show nothing of meditation, adoration, or even of conventional petition. The mood is "won't-be-denied, won't-stop-asking." Obviously they portray only one aspect of prayer, but it is one that has its place. And we should note that the one concludes with Jesus saying, "And yet, when the Son of Man comes, will he find faith on earth?" (18:8).

The same quality of urgency, and even of harshness, characterizes the other parables on this Jerusalem journey. There is the story of a fig tree that has been unproductive; the landowner wants to be done with it, but the gardener appeals for one more chance (13:6-9). Another story tells of the rich fool who, thinking he has it made, asks no questions about tomorrow (12:16-21). Then there is the story of the dishonest manager who protects his future by clever manipulating (16:1-9). It is a peculiar story, one that has frustrated scholars and nonscholars alike for centuries. Whatever might be said of it, one thing is sure: this story has the same mood of urgency that we are noticing in this section. It is as if our Lord were saying that times will get so bad that we will be forced to extremes in our stretch to survive.

In one sense, the two Lukan stories in Chapter 15—the lost coin and the lost son—have a very different mood. They are marked by the love of the seekers, the woman

Our author says that in a sense, the parables of the lost coin and the lost sheep were a rebuke to the Pharisees and the scribes. Explain why you agree or disagree. Someone has said that good preaching ought to comfort the afflicted and afflict the comfortable. Is that true in Luke 15? Explain.

and the father, and by grand celebration in the hour of finding. Nevertheless, when we consider the persons to whom Jesus was immediately directing these two stories—the Pharisees and scribes—we realize that for them, the stories were a rebuke. The secondary audience of tax collectors and sinners would find the stories comforting, but the scribes and Pharisees had to realize that they were being severely reprimanded.

All of which is to say that Luke, who is perhaps the gentlest and most sensitive of the Gospel writers, conveys better than any other the insistence, the urgency, and even the anger of our Lord. But this is no contradiction in character. The person who goes into the ghetto or some remote rural area to teach is motivated by love for students and for learning, but is also driven by hatred for ignorance and for what ignorance does to people. One cannot love passionately without despising that which hurts the beloved.

Whatever the urgency of this road to Jerusalem, Jesus is never so hurried as to neglect people. And to make the point still more dramatic, in most instances Jesus was giving time to people who were otherwise pretty generally

> **Whatever the urgency of this road to Jerusalem, Jesus is never so hurried as to neglect people.**

overlooked. He stopped to cleanse ten lepers who were "keeping their distance" (17:11-19). It is wonderfully ironic that nine of them, in turn, did not have time to thank him! He took time to bless children, when his disciples—at this moment very time-conscious—tried to shunt the children aside (18:15-17). He healed a blind beggar, whom others were trying to quiet to the point of being missed (18:35-43). And he stopped not only to talk with the despised (though very successful) tax collector, Zaccheus, but also to invite himself to the man's house for dinner (19:1-10). Of course none of this should surprise us, because the end-issue of Jesus' urgency was people. He was intent on getting to Jerusalem because it was there that he would make his ultimate sacrifice for people. If he had pushed people aside in his hurry to reach Jerusalem, he would have been quite inconsistent.

Judgment, Crucifixion, and Resurrection

Now it is the end. Or perhaps we should say, the beginning. It is for this reason that Jesus has come into the world. No wonder he has hurried to get to Jerusalem! He enters the city in triumph, though it is triumph of a peculiar kind, with Jesus riding on a ridiculous little donkey colt. And while the believers—probably a somewhat motley crew—spread cloaks in his path and shout his praises, the real power brokers insist that he put a stop to the celebration. No wonder, then, that Jesus pauses to weep over the city as he ponders its coming disasters.

There are questions and discussions and lessons drawn from the scene, like the widow with her all-out gift (21:1-4). Then we read that a plot has developed and that one of Jesus' own close-knit company, Judas, is part of it. Meanwhile, Jesus proceeds with plans for the Passover and then with the celebration that Christians now observe as Holy Communion. We have known all along that the disciples are as human as we are, but now they go out of their way to prove it as they argue among themselves as to "which of them was to be regarded as the greatest" (22:24). We know of course that the shadow of the cross is hanging over their conversation, so we see their remarks as an obscenity. But they are only engaging themselves, as we

humans so often do, in excited one-upmanship. Then Jesus prays, with an intensity that we cannot grasp, because we do not conceive of the issues at stake in Jesus' struggle of soul.

While Jesus is still remonstrating with his disciples over their spiritual ineptness, the betrayal and arrest take place. We see a kaleidoscope of events, surrealistic in the disdain for goodness and humanity. He is "treated . . . with contempt and mocked" (23:11); but Luke tells us—ironically, I think—that Herod and Pilate became friends that day, apparently as a result of their common involvement in injustice. When we think how many millions of words have been written about the crucifixion of Jesus, we are astonished at the few words Luke (or any other Gospel writer) invests in the story. We see rejection, humiliation, human bestiality, and suffering. We realize that while the human suffering is intense, the ultimate measure is spiritual; our Lord is taking upon himself the sin of the world.

Luke includes one detail missing from the other Gospels, the conversion of one of the thieves

Many persons have been brutally treated, in both personal and religious persecution over the centuries. What makes the suffering of Jesus uniquely intense (Luke 23:6-32)?

Why, do you think, did it mean so much to the disciples to see Jesus eat a piece of fish?

who died with Jesus. It is magnificently appropriate to the Christian story in general, and to Luke's Gospel in particular, that the first person to come—both literally and spiritually—to the cross is a person so obviously lost and despised; a deathbed conversion, even!

And then, Easter! A few women, loyal in their love even though without hope, coming early, with "the spices that they had prepared" (24:1). Their response to the Resurrection is bewilderment; and when they report to the men, the men see their words as "an idle tale" (24:11).

The two men (one of them Luke?) who walk to Emmaus look like the lonely souls of all the ages who are looking for they know not what and, while they fumble their way, are joined by the Savior. Is he real? Their joy is mixed with disbelief (24:41). And then, he eats a piece of broiled fish "in their presence" (24:43). The disciples are not convinced by aura or presence or words, but by his chewing on a piece of fish. So earthly, so divine; so wondrous, so common. Such is our eternal faith. No wonder, then, that in time they are "continually in the temple blessing God" (24:53). Life is ecstatic with promise.

Luke in Particular

Luke chooses to include in his record so many incidents and teachings that are not in the other Gospels; and when he handles the same material as another Gospel writer, he so often introduces nuances of his own. Several matters are especially significant.

Everyone. Luke's Gospel is wonderfully inclusive. Where Matthew's genealogy of Jesus goes back to Abraham, emphasizing his Jewishness, Luke goes back to Adam, thus connecting with everyone. When Simeon, the devout Jew, celebrates Jesus' birth, he includes the phrase, "a light for revelation to the Gentiles" (2:32). When Luke reports Jesus' sermon in Nazareth, he includes our Lord's reference to two Gentiles who were party to miracles even though there were "many

Our author chooses three Lukan points of emphasis: *everyone, unwanted,* and *women.* What, do you think, is outstanding about these emphases? From your own reading of Luke, what other points seem to stand out?

How does Luke help us see that Jesus is for everyone? Review several of the Scriptures in this section and discuss how Christians today bring the gospel to everyone.

. . . in Israel" who might have received these blessings (4:25-27). All four Gospel writers quote part of Isaiah 40 when they introduce the ministry of John the Baptist, but only Luke continues to the all-embracing phrase, "and all flesh shall see the salvation of God" (3:6). And only Luke carries Jesus' words, "Then people will come from east and west, from north and south, and will eat in the kingdom of God" (13:29).

Luke spells "everyone" by specific attention to the people Jews particularly resented: the Samaritans. He alone tells us the story of the good Samaritan (10:25-37). Only Luke's Gospel reports the healing of the ten lepers, with the particular fact that it is only the Samaritan who returns to give thanks (17:11-19). But Luke is a faithful historian and does not whitewash his data. When Jesus begins his journey to Jerusalem, a village of Samaritans will not receive him "because his face was set toward Jerusalem" (9:53). Luke does not slip into the kind of easy sentimentalism that would picture Samaritans as perfect folks who simply have not had a chance. They, too, are sinners, and they, too, can be narrow and close-minded.

Unwanted. Luke has a gift for those who are forgotten, ignored, or simply not wanted. This mood first appears, though somewhat subtly, in the story of the shepherds—quintessential outsiders! Yet their Christmas invitation is delivered by an angel. Then, when Jesus is presented in the Temple, Mary's offering for purification is the one that the poor used (Luke 2:24; Leviticus 12:8). In a culture that was inclined to feel that prosperity was a sign of God's favor, the poor were naturally suspect. But not to Luke.

Women. Luke says so much about the place of women in Jesus' life and ministry. He tells us about the wonderful saint, Anna (2:36-38), and of Jesus' relationship with Mary and Martha (10:38-42). Two of his parables have women as lead characters (15:8-10; 18:1-8); the second story is an especially fascinating depiction.

It seems to me that authors sometimes say the most in subtle ways, so I am very taken with the way Luke dates the angel's visit to Mary. He has been telling us about Elizabeth's pregnancy and how for five months she has been in seclusion. Then he continues, "In the sixth month the angel Gabriel was sent by God to a town in Galilee called Nazareth" (1:26). How delightful, that the calendar of God's visitation is measured, not by the usual references to kings and public officials, but by the ancient measure of a woman's calendar, by the development of her pregnancy! It is a touch that is at once wonderfully human, wonderfully feminine, and graciously divine.

3

LUKE DIAGNOSES THE HUMAN CONDITION

Diagnoses of the human condition have rarely been as plentiful as at this turn of the millennium. In other times such evaluating has been left pretty much to philosophers, whether those by profession or by virtue of age. But now the diagnosticians are on every side: political pundits, government figures, university professors, preachers, poets, playwrights, mystics, and bartenders.

Even the most time-bound person would acknowledge that people like Socrates and the prophet Isaiah, though they lived centuries ago, can nevertheless add something to our modern knowledge of the human condition; and the writers of the Psalms have provided us with nothing less than a basic text in human psychology. So what might Luke, in the first century, have to offer?

A Lover of People

Luke had a head start in understanding our human condition because he was so clearly a people-person. He treats almost everyone sympathetically. Perhaps this is the doctor in Luke. Physicians, by the nature of their work, see people without adornment.

Luke shows his fascination with the human race in the parables that are exclusively his. Where Matthew tells us that the kingdom of heaven is like a mustard seed, a pearl, or seed sown in a field, Luke involves us with poignant human scenes. Obviously, when Matthew tells about the seed sown in a field he is also telling about a sower; when he tells of a pearl of great price he speaks also of a passionate buyer; and when the kingdom of heaven is like

In what ways can you identify Luke as a "people-person"?

What traits of the human condition do you identify in the parables mentioned in this section? Which parable is your favorite? Why?

yeast there is a woman mixing it with her flour. The central figure in each story, however, is an object. Not so with the parables that Luke chooses to emphasize; they center on human beings.

If we were to take the time, we could note the qualities of anguish, joy, and recognition in Luke's stories, including the parable of the rich fool (Luke 12:13-21) and the story of the rich man and Lazarus (16:19-31). But even in haste, let me pause at Luke's two great parables on prayer, because they give us still another insight into Luke as a people-person. Specifically, it is a picture of Luke's sense of humor.

In the story of the man who has a late-night guest and who then proceeds to awaken his neighbor in his quest for food, the scene is hilarious. Both men are absurdly frantic: the one, because he cannot bear to tell his guest that he cannot feed him, and the other, because he is afraid he will awaken his whole family (11:5-13). The same quality comes through in the story of the widow who will not let go of the unjust judge (18:1-8). One can see this feisty little woman camping out at every turn until the judge has lost all of his dignity and is driven simply by his desire to be done with this woman. Jesus obviously had fun telling these stories, and Luke enjoys relating them.

Our Human Condition: Lost

Luke knows that we human beings are sinners, but he has his own favorite words for describing us. We are lost. No place is it said more effectively than in Chapter 15. It is Luke's report on the controversy that constantly existed between Jesus and the religious leaders of his day.

These were the people who ought really to have embraced Jesus most favorably, because they were the ones who wanted so earnestly to see God's will done in the world. But at the same time, unfortunately, they were so certain about how God would do this will that they could not distinguish between God's will and their perception of God's will. They had invested so much

What contemporary figure of speech compares with Luke's term *lost* for defining our human condition? Does Luke's term apply as well today as it did in the first century? Review the three parables of the lost coin, sheep, and son (Luke 15).

Why, do you think, were the scribes and Pharisees so apparently out of touch with "sinners"? Why were they so isolated from the situation of "common folk"? Of what sins might they have been guilty?

of their own ego in their understanding of God that they could not tolerate having that understanding questioned. That is always something of a danger for us religious people.

So although probably many of the scribes and Pharisees felt as Nicodemus did, that no one could work the miracles Jesus worked unless God was with him (John 3:2), they were troubled that Jesus was not their kind of person. Especially, that he was so often surrounded by publicans and sinners. Even worse, Jesus accepted them and ate with them (Luke 15:2). It was particularly to this group of religious critics, scribes and Pharisees, that Jesus addressed the three parables that are recorded in Luke 15.

In each instance, we have one defining element: lostness. We have a lost coin, a lost sheep, and a lost son; or perhaps, more correctly, two lost sons. Perhaps there is some progression of responsibility in the lostness. A lost coin seems not to be blamed at all, because what can a coin do to protect itself from being lost? A lost sheep bears somewhat more responsibility, because even though an unreasoning beast, it did allow itself to become separated from the rest of the flock. The younger son is still more responsible, because he chose to

God is One who pursues us and who pleads for a chance to reason with us for our salvation.

collect an early inheritance and to leave home. As for the elder son, he stayed at home; and yet he seemed unaware of his father's spirit and was as lost from the character of his father as if he had himself wasted his substance in riotous living. And as the one (perhaps like the scribes and Pharisees) most in a position to understand home, he is probably the one most responsible in his own lostness.

In every case the defining word is *lost*. The emphasis is not on the badness of the coin, the sheep, or the sons, but the lostness. Mind you, in the end the result is the same. But the image is significantly different.

In any event, Jesus is asking the scribes and the Pharisees to look compassionately on the human condition. We are lost creatures. How could these religious leaders have lost sight of this fact, and how could they claim to represent God and not be sensitive to our lostness? If God is One who pursues us and who pleads for a chance to reason with us for our salvation; indeed, if God is One who sends prophets to make the divine will clear, and who before that provides the people with a system of sacrifices and holy days; well then, this is a God who loves our human race and who recognizes that we are lost. How is it that these who knew the Scriptures so well could so completely miss the quality of the God whom they quite earnestly followed? Clearly, they were quite like the older brother in the family parable: a person who could live so close to his father physically (ritually?), yet never grasp his spirit. They demonstrated that one can live in the precincts of the father's house, yet be a prodigal.

What Jesus taught by parable, as recorded in Luke 15, he taught by action in his meeting with Zaccheus (19:1-10). The circumstances surrounding the two instances are quite similar. Zaccheus belonged to the despised profession of tax collector. When he went to extreme efforts to see Jesus, Jesus invited himself to Zaccheus's home. In doing so, Jesus knew that he would evoke criticism, since Zaccheus was by common definition both a sinner and a national traitor. Sure enough, the criticism came. It must have been rather general criticism, because while the comments in Luke 15 are said to have come from the Pharisees and scribes, we are told in this case that "all who saw it began to grumble" (Luke 19:7). That sounds as if even the "commonly" good people were upset, perhaps because they were among those who felt they had been defrauded by Zaccheus, or perhaps because there is a kind of degree of badness among sinners, and all of us are always hoping to find someone who is a bit worse than we are. In Zaccheus, most ordinary sinners found someone deliciously beneath themselves.

But Jesus announced that salvation had come that day to the household of Zaccheus. Then he spoke what are, next to John 3:16, perhaps the loveliest words in the Bible: "For the Son of Man came to seek out and to save the lost" (Luke 19:10). Here Jesus defines his whole divine mission in one word: *lost*. It is for this reason that he came; not to teach, to heal, to cast out demons, or to confound the Pharisees, but to seek and to save the lost.

Zaccheus (Luke 19:1-10) and the dying thief (Luke 23:39-43: had been lost, but Jesus found them. What happened? How could their stories apply to you?

We do not often hear the term *sin* used today. How do we describe it? What term might a psychiatrist use? a sociologist? a political analyst? a sports writer describing an athlete who is frequently in trouble?

It is beautifully appropriate, then, that Luke's Gospel should include the story of the conversion of the dying thief (23:39-43). From a human vantage point, no one could have seemed more lost than this person who was now an outcast of society, condemned by law, and on the verge of death. What chance is there of redemption; and with so little time left, why bother? But Jesus assures the man that he will soon have a place in paradise. So Jesus' final ministry act, as Luke reports it, is finding a lost soul. It is as if the church has begun its mission at this point, a mission that Luke will continue reporting in the Book of Acts.

And yet it is very important, as we see Luke's emphasis on our human lostness, that we not slip into an easy sentimentality. *Lost* is a more compassionate word than *sinner*, but the end result is the same; and I do not think Luke would want us to forget that fact. He was not trying to be politically correct in describing humans as lost; rather, he was seeking to dramatize the nature of our tragedy.

Perhaps he was also trying to put both an urgency and a heightened compassion in the work of those who have already been found. If someone is lost, we cannot be content until they are found. Nor can we think that we solve the

> **Compassion ought to be our defining quality of ministry.**

problem by redefining what *lost* means.

Lost is lost, for all of our semantics. The very starkness and directness of the word ought to impel us. But at the same time, it should save us from making moral judgments. Compassion ought to be our defining quality of ministry.

Our Human Condition: Hoping, Dreaming, Yearning

We are a people who are uncertain and searching. This is appropriate to the sense deep within us that we are meant to be better than we are. The Bible says that we were born for an Eden. Having lost it, we are constantly on a search, constantly intent, usually uncertain.

Luke opens his Gospel with a picture of hoping, yearning people who have hoped for so long that their hopes have grown tired. Zechariah and Elizabeth are among the best of persons: "righteous before God, living blamelessly according to all the commandments and regulations of the Lord" (1:6). But they had been unable to have children; and in a culture where children were looked upon as a heritage from the Lord, those who could not conceive were somehow suspect. If they were truly good, why had God not made them fruitful? How long is it before hope, deferred, grows sick?

Idealism makes us want to see Elizabeth and Zechariah maintaining the stiff upper lip of bright hope, but such an expectation is unrealistic. I think, rather, that they had allowed their hope to become reconciled to reality. So it is that when the angel tells Zechariah that he and Elizabeth will conceive, Zechariah reminds the angel of the problems they face—problems that they had no doubt discussed endlessly in family hours. And Zechariah does so in the face of a remarkable angelic visit and message. If I read his message rightly, I hear an undertone that says, "I've been fooled by my hopes too many times over the years. I want some proof this time, before I venture again into that speculative sea of hope."

You and I are instinctively hopeful creatures. Perhaps it is part of our heritage from Eden. Something in us insists that things not only ought to be perfect, they actually can be. So we keep hoping and dreaming and yearning. And for believers, the quality of hope is deepened. Zechariah and Elizabeth were an extraordinarily devout couple; their piety was real and consistent. But even the most devout can lose hope, or at the least, can convince themselves that their hope has been unreasonable, or that perhaps it is not in the will of God. I think this couple had come to such a place.

The shepherds, to my mind, portray another kind of dreaming and hoping. They were simply doing their job, "living in the fields, keeping watch over their flock by night" (2:8). It was their good fortune that they were doing so "in that region," because it was in that region that history took its sharpest turn, its eternal one. If I know anything about working people, from growing up in a neighborhood of working class people, it is that dreams come to be scaled down; or perhaps, more correctly, never get stimulated to grandiose possibilities.

From your own experience, do you think "we are a people who are uncertain and searching"? Explain.

Compare the hopes and dreams of Elizabeth with those of the shepherds (Luke 1:1–2:18), as you understand them. To which do you relate most naturally? Whom have you known who might compare with either party, in their hopes and dreams?

What might have been the yearnings of the bent-over woman (Luke 13:10-17) and the man who had dropsy (14:1-6)? What do those yearnings teach us?

But God's visitation is not limited by our human experiences, nor by our cultural boundaries. Now and again, God visits extravagant dreams upon persons who have modest expectations. The angelic visit to the shepherds is pure grace. They were not, as far as the Scriptures indicate, seekers; they were not, that is, like Zechariah and Elizabeth nor like Simeon and Anna. I doubt that they entertained great dreams.

God's gracious kindness must visit even those who, through generations of deprivation, have lost their capacity for extensive longing. Those shepherds must have been something like that—persons with little obvious capacity to dream. And into their world, the angels came with a song. This is Luke's wondrous declaration of the reaching grace of God.

Perhaps this is one of the most telling qualities in Luke's book. He understands that every human being is capable of dreaming and that the degree to which those dreams are expressed is no indication of either the capacity to dream or of the depth of the longing. We often think of the poets as our dreamers, but this is only because poets do better with words. Get the repairman who

> **Even our obvious longings have complex depths that only God's Spirit can explore.**

comes to your home, or the taxi driver, or the hairdresser to speak from the soul, and you discover the depth of their dreams and longings.

And Luke caught this. He shows it in Simeon and Anna, who wait at the Temple daily for the revelation of God's Messiah; they are old enough that they might be told to leave such dreams to those who can see them fulfilled. But Simeon is willing to make his exit only after he can say, "my eyes have seen your salvation" (2:30). We know that even the seemingly thoughtless crowds are yearning, because they flock into the wilderness to hear John the Baptist preach, then ask to be baptized by him (3:3-10).

Sometimes the yearning is obvious, as in the instance of the widow at Nain who has lost her only son. But even our obvious longings have complex depths that only God's Spirit can explore. And you feel that peculiar, mixed pathos of our yearning when Jesus is at the home of Mary and Martha. Mary understands her yearning well enough to seek its fulfillment, while her sister Martha thinks she is quite happy just preparing a meal for Jesus (in her world of kitchen-security) until she realizes what she may be missing (10:38-42).

Of course it is easy to see the yearning of the woman who is bowed groundward by a crippling infirmity (13:10-17) and that of a man suffering from dropsy (14:1-6). Luke tells these two stories to show us Jesus healing on the sabbath. Jesus' critics feel that healing can just as well be postponed a day, to keep the sabbath free of labor. Jesus seems by his action to say that the sabbath has no better fulfillment than the meeting of our human yearning. After all, the sabbath is itself God's gift to satisfy the yearning for rest, so why not extend its domain—and as soon as possible!

Luke's Gospel ends with two fine instances of human yearning. One comes at the moment of death, as a thief who is being crucified with Jesus pleads for a place in our Lord's kingdom. Who would think that such an unsavory character would have such exalted dreams? Those who gave him the death sentence obviously thought the world would be better off without him. Yet Luke makes clear that this lonely man recognizes Jesus for who he is. At that moment, captive to death, Jesus looks less like a king than at any time since the poignantly simple setting of his birth. But the thief has the (unsought) advantage of being so close to death that his vision is dramatically clear. He dares to voice his yearning, and the Master gladly promises an answer.

Then, we have the two disciples who are en route to Emmaus (24:13-35). Since their experience is part of the Easter story, it would be theologically appropriate to say that they were yearning for eternal life, but I doubt that this was their primary concern. At the moment, they wanted only to get some understanding of dreams that had gone utterly awry. "But we had hoped," they explained, "that he was the one to redeem Israel" (24:21). Perhaps nothing is worse than this, that our dreams can be shattered so shamelessly as to make it absurd that we ever entertained them.

But of course is not this, at least in a measure, what Easter is about? If there is any ultimate crusher of dreams, it is death. At

---

Luke reports that one of the crucified thieves repented, while Matthew says they both mocked Jesus. Develop an imaginary scenario as to what the repentant thief might have experienced earlier in life that would cause him to be more open to conversion than the other thief.

Have you had experience of engaging in conversation about deep longings? What did you discover? What is it that you long for the most?

that point, all the dreams come to an end, all yearnings are made pointless. It is one of the fine touches of Luke's Gospel that he pictures human yearning, at first frustrated and then fulfilled, at the scene of Resurrection.

What Kind of People Were They?

So what kind of people were these persons in Luke's Gospel, these people whose human condition Luke so ably analyzes? One is likely to think that Luke's Gospel is made up only of assorted rogues. I rejoice that Luke had such a heart for rogues and that he conveys to us so well the love Jesus felt for such persons. But human beings are human beings. When Luke puts together a rogues' gallery, I easily find a place there. I recall the sociology professor who warned us, as our class began a study of abnormal psychology, that we would almost surely see ourselves in each description of abnormality; because, he explained, what we call abnormal is nothing other than our usual conditions writ large. Our hymnody is replete with songs that number us among the needy and unrepentant, the yearning and the hopeful, the blessed and the saved.

How Are Luke's People Like Us?

Luke's people may not wear clothes with designer labels, and they may not be familiar with fax machines and cafe society; but they are our soul kin. When I read Luke's Gospel, I realize I am looking at a photo gallery of my neighborhood, indeed, a snapshot collection of the events and longings, the bemusements and bewilderments, of my own soul.

At our best, we are like Zechariah and Elizabeth, Simeon and Anna. Those of us who are engaged in this study are probably seekers of long standing. Our credentials are not as venerable as the four persons I have just mentioned, but they go back a ways. Some of us have been seeking since childhood Sunday school; and when we recall our earliest longings, we think that probably we were seeking before our conscious memories. To long is human, and to long for God is humanity at its best, its most

What does it mean to you that Luke and Jesus "had such a heart for rogues"?

Do you think of any hymn or popular song that recognizes that all human beings are in need of God's grace? What key lyrics identify the human condition?

basic, and its most primitive. The longing for God can be refined by music, literature, and philosophy; but there always remains in it something of the infant cry or the pathos of a lost child. We are seekers. It is our native state, our truest heart. And no one describes our state better than Luke.

At our worst, we are like the Pharisee, in Jesus' wonderful Temple scene (18:9-14). We are always looking for someone who is a bit less spiritual than we are, someone more qualified to be the chief of sinners. This was an easy search for the Pharisee, because the publican had the bad taste to come to the place of prayer at the same hour. Besides, the Pharisee was a more measurably good person than most of us. I tithe, but not as scrupulously as he did; I fast, but rarely and comfortably. If anyone is ever qualified to be spiritually condescending (and of course those two words constitute a scathing oxymoron), it would be the Pharisee.

But even without the Pharisee's qualifications, I sometimes lean closer to him than to the publican. Sometimes, momentarily, I think I understand why God has been so good to me. Sometimes I marvel that I tithe when some in my profession do not; or I wonder how it is that people can preach, yet clearly have an indifferent devotional life. And of course I am suspicious that so many Christians can be so taken with the material and the secular. Because I have read Jesus' parable, I do not mention these matters to my Lord in my temple prayers, but I think about them sometimes. I am kin to the Pharisee.

And I know many who are like Zaccheus. They have gotten the brass ring, and they wonder now why it does not fit. Having come, as Zaccheus did, to the chief place in their profession or business or community, they keep watching the parade go by and keep wondering why they cannot see Jesus (by whatever name they are calling him) when their clothes are so fine, their position so eminent, their wealth so secure. So many of us are kin to Zaccheus.

Ah, Dr. Luke, thank you for telling us what manner of persons we are and for telling us of our ultimate Healer.

Do you know someone who seems to you like a modern Elizabeth, Anna, Zechariah, or Simeon? Do you know anyone who has lived with a vital faith for a long lifetime in Simeon and Anna's style? In what ways have they impressed or inspired you?

Review Luke 18:9-14. Do you relate to either the Pharisee or the tax collector? Who? Why? (Be as honest and as specific as you can.)

4

LUKE TELLS US ABOUT JESUS CHRIST

10/3

I suppose it is only coincidence that the four Gospels were written just a decade or two before Plutarch and Suetonius established the art of biography as we know it. The timing is fascinating because the Gospels are ultimately the best known, most widely read, and certainly the most widely translated of any biographies ever written.

This, of course, is altogether astonishing. Plutarch chose to write biographies of famous Greeks and Romans, providing material for several of Shakespeare's plays. Suetonius also wrote about people of power, particularly the Caesars. But the Gospels tell the story of a man who never held public power and never aspired to, though he was executed as a threat to Caesar. He was born to common folk who would be lost in the masses of such persons if their names were not associated with his. He grew up in a backwash of a village, the kind of town that would make some people try to write it out of their history. He remained in that town until he was thirty years old, then began to teach. He had no school or classroom, and his major body of students—just twelve men—was made up of a quite unimpressive conglomerate of persons. Others listened to his teachings and some of them—including especially some women—followed very earnestly whenever they had the opportunity. But most people who knew him as a teacher heard him only now and then, as a traveling lecturer. In his lectures he drew upon the most ordinary materials—lilies of the field, birds of the air, women hunting for lost coins, a man sowing seed, a merchant looking for a priceless pearl.

Yet somehow crowds were drawn to him. Many came because he healed the sick and others because they enjoyed watching him debate the establishment. But mostly, it seems that people were simply drawn to him. He was perhaps the most popular dinner guest in Palestine, and his invitations came from the widest possible variety of hosts and hostesses. Religious authorities became more and more nervous about him. Some of them admired his transparency of character and the quality of his teaching, yet they were uneasy as to where it would all end, especially since they did not like the way masses of people—including socially undesirable people— were drawn to him.

So after no more than three years of his teaching and healing ventures, his enemies brought him to a quick, unjust trial and execution, including base public humiliation. That should have been the end of him. After all, what was there to build on? Who cares, really, that a teacher of no recognized school, himself trained by an unknown village rabbi, has wandered in a tiny country for three years, has died ignominiously, and has left behind no obvious organization?

And yet, by the time Luke writes his biography, sometime within a generation or two after Jesus' death, he tells us that "many" have already written this story! Jesus is not a Caesar or a member of any royal court. He has no distinguished followers. Those who praise his name are intermittently sought out for imprisonment and even execution. But with it all, more people keep wanting to write their remembrances of him, and vast, vast numbers want to read and hear those remembrances. So without the advantage of the printing press and without anything resembling a contemporary public relations structure (indeed, without anything resembling any kind of structure), people struggled to copy his story by hand, and to circulate it in person.

But Is It Biography?

And that is where Luke comes in. But are the Gospels really biographies? Some say they are not. One author has said that Luke calls his work, not a biography, but a gospel; that is, good news. But that begs the question. The

How would you define biography? List some biographies that you have read over several years; how are they different in their approach?

Can one be an evangelist and also a biographer? Can you think of some secular instances of persons who are earnest advocates for a given personality and also have written a biography of the person?

What does our author mean by his term *campaign biographies*? Is this a good description of the Gospels?

subject of Luke's biography is the good news, and to tell his story is to unfold the good news.

Yes, Luke—like Matthew, Mark, and John—is a special kind of biographer. He is, indeed, an evangelist, a bearer of good news. The Gospel writers are, in a peculiar sense, campaign biographers. They are writing documents that are intended to persuade readers and hearers to vote for the kingdom of God, though not to get Jesus "elected." That issue is already, eternally settled. It is that by voting for Jesus the readers and hearers will enter the Kingdom with Jesus Christ as their Lord.

Jesus Christ and the Emperors

Luke meets this issue head-on. When he is ready to tell us about the birth of Jesus, he reminds us that Joseph and Mary are in Bethlehem when Jesus is born because a decree has gone out from Emperor Augustus "that all the world should be registered."

Furthermore, this registration "was taken while Quirinius was governor of Syria" (Luke 2:1, 2). Then, when it is time to tell of the beginning of John the Baptist's ministry, which sets the stage for Jesus' baptism and ministry, Luke again gives us a historical setting through the names of rulers. He lists six persons, beginning with Emperor Tiberius, the successor to Augustus, three provincial rulers (Herod, Philip, and Lysanias), and two religious rulers (Annas and Caiaphas).

In doing this, Luke is on the one hand a careful historian, letting us know precisely the time of events in Jesus' life—and making clear that Jesus is a historical figure, not a myth. But it seems to me that he is also throwing down a kind of gauntlet. Jesus is contesting with the rulers of this earth for the souls of men and women.

In the first-century world there was a growing cult of emperor worship that offered salvation through the Roman Caesar. The emperor was referred to by such terms as savior, son of God, and

How were the events in Jesus' birth described? How do we date significant events today (other than by specific dates)? How can the timing of those events affect what and how we remember things?

How were Roman emperors described by many of their followers in the centuries surrounding the time of Jesus?

How did this common attitude make Jesus an issue in the first-century world? Where in our contemporary world might this same issue arise?

Lord and God. People spoke of the emperor as bringing in the golden age. Miracle stories circulated widely. One said that Augustus made withered trees come to life and healed the sick. Hadrian was said to have produced rain in a parched area of Africa. Nature was so subservient to Domitian that elephants bowed down to him, and the moon and stars stood still in order to stare at him. Domitian's pardons were called *gospel,* the very word used in the New Testament (*The Layman's Bible Commentary,* Volume 18, pages 8–9).

So for the average person in the Roman Empire, Jesus was a lively issue. To call him Lord and Savior was, at the least, to diminish the emperor and his role. Luke, the most politically sophisticated of the Gospel writers, makes this point clear. Where Matthew emphasizes Jesus' role as the fulfillment of the Hebrew Scriptures, where Mark portrays him as one marvelously in command, and where John exalts him as the Word of God since before creation, Luke puts particular content into "the things about which you have been instructed" (1:4). Luke impels his readers to a choice—the announced rulers of this world, or Jesus.

> **To call Jesus Lord and Savior was, at the least, to diminish the emperor and his role.**

Human and Divine

How did Luke perceive Jesus? In truth, all of the Gospels present both the humanity and the divinity of Jesus, and each Gospel has its own way of emphasizing both elements in our Lord. This surely should not surprise us. After all, this is part of the glory of the individual Gospels, that each establishes its own vantage point for telling the story and therefore each has its own emphasis. And since Christian doctrine has traditionally insisted that Jesus was both human and divine, we should expect to find evidence for each aspect of his personality.

Luke gives even more attention than Matthew to the unique nature of Jesus' conception and birth. Both writers make clear that Mary's conception of Jesus was by an act of the Holy Spirit. In Matthew's report, a distressed Joseph is told by an angel that he need not fear because "the child conceived in [Mary] is from the Holy Spirit" (Matthew 1:20), and that the child's name will be Jesus, "for he will save his people from their sins" (Matthew 1:21).

Luke goes into much more detail. It is partly a matter of what I describe as Luke's human interest style. But it is also more theologically specific. The unique significance of Jesus is heightened by the background story of John the Baptist's conception—as if Luke were saying that Jesus is so special that the one who will introduce him is also special, though in a lesser degree. No ordinary prophet with an ordinary birth is sufficient for this task!

Then Luke tells us of the angel Gabriel's visit to Mary, and of their intense dialogue. Particularly, he reports the very human problem Mary faced: How can she have a child when she is a virgin? Luke wants no misunderstanding here; Mary's pregnancy, when it occurs, will be outside the realm of human explanation. The angel's answer is direct, clear, and beyond negotiation: "The Holy Spirit will come upon you, and the power of the Most High will overshadow you; therefore the child to be born will be holy; he will be called Son of God" (Luke 1:35). Mary's answer—

"Here am I, the servant of the Lord; let it be with me according to your word" (1:38) is often cited for its beauty of submission. I admire Mary's spirit, but I am also impressed that the angel had not left her much room for debate.

But Luke is not done. He now tells of Mary's visit to Elizabeth, and in this unfolding he tells us of Mary's magnificent song. With the Holy Spirit upon her, Mary stretches her young arms to embrace the history of her people and the exalted purposes of God. And there is still more.

Now Luke takes us back to the unfolding story of John the Baptist, and once more reports a miracle—this time of Zechariah regaining his speech. When, months later, the baby Jesus is born, shepherds are visited by an angel, and then "a multitude of the heavenly host" (2:13) add their awesome touch. Luke wants us to understand that while this

From your knowledge of the four Gospels, how true is it that each one portrays Jesus as both divine and human? As you read, do you sense that Luke emphasizes one over the other?

List the elements in Jesus' birth story (including the story of John the Baptist's birth) that might be considered out of the ordinary.

Are we, in our century, more objective than the people of Luke's time? What cultural and intellectual factors influence our thinking?

Our author says that the humanness of Jesus is as important as the divinity. Do you agree? Why?

birth was generally overlooked on earth, except for a visit from some of society's least esteemed, it was spectacular news in heaven.

As for the particular issue of the divine conception through a virgin, it is important to remember that this was not a keystone issue in the early Christian preaching. When we read the sermons in the Book of Acts, we find that the watershed issue was Jesus' resurrection; his birth is not mentioned. The supreme issue of his birth is not a matter of biology, but of divine intent. Luke and the other New Testament writers want us to know that Jesus came as God's invasion of planet earth. He was born as God's Son and Messiah. His story is not that of a baby who rose from obscurity to astonishing success, but of God humbly coming in flesh in order to reach the daughters and sons of earth.

John will tell us later that Jesus was "the Word [that] was with God, and the Word was God," even from the beginning (John 1:1). Paul will tell us that "in him all the fullness of God was pleased to dwell" (Colossians 1:19). The author of Revelation says that he has "the keys of Death and of Hades" (Revelation 1:18). These statements stretch us to the limits of both our philosophical perception and our faith capacity. But in reality they are nothing more than extensions of Luke's story—that when Jesus Christ came into the world, it was a divine act. When you read the theology of Ephesians, Colossians, and Hebrews, you wonder how Luke could tell it so simply; sometimes, indeed, almost matter-of-factly.

But the matter-of-factness is appropriate, because divine as Jesus may be, he is also human. Luke never plays down that fact, and why should he? The humanness is just as important to the story as the divinity. So in Luke's Gospel, as we indicated earlier, the term Jesus seems to use most often in self-description is "Son of Man." No one can say exactly what content Jesus was putting into this term. It was used previously by the prophet Ezekiel, but there is no indication that Jesus

What significance do you see in Jesus' describing himself as the "Son of Man"? Can you see any factors in Luke's Gospel that cause him to emphasize these references where other Gospel writers do not?

Review the passage of Jesus in Gethsemane (Luke 22:39-46). What of Jesus' humanity and divinity do you see there? What is instructive about that experience for us?

was harking back to Ezekiel in his usage. I think that in using this term, Jesus was choosing directly to identify himself with our human state.

Luke is always candid in portraying the humanness of Jesus. He shows his impatience with the scribes and Pharisees, and also with Herod. He tells us twice of Jesus' sorrow, even unto tears, over Jerusalem. Luke's portrayal of Jesus' struggle in Gethsemane (Luke 22:39-46) does not make as much of the failure of the disciples as do Matthew and Mark, but it is more vivid in telling us of Jesus' own anguish. It becomes so great, Luke says, that an angel comes to minister to him. Jesus' suffering is so intense that his perspiration becomes like blood; some scholars note that Luke uses a medical term to describe this condition. I think it is probably significant that—as Luke tells it—before Jesus begins his Gethsemane prayer, he urges his disciples to pray lest they enter into temptation. It is almost as if he is projecting on them the struggle that at that moment he contemplates for himself.

I believe it is fair to say that

Luke is not uncomfortable with either the divinity or the humanity of Jesus. It may well be that he would wonder why some find it so hard to accept, and to balance, the two.

Luke Emphasizes Compassion

As we have noticed before, Luke gives special attention to certain elements in the character of Jesus. I think that a sensitive portrait artist could paint pictures of Jesus from each of the Gospels that would show us, in the very lines of Jesus' face, whether this is the Jesus of Matthew, Mark, Luke, or John. And in some ways, Luke's portrait would be the easiest to develop, because his points of emphasis are so distinctive.

The one compelling point is the quality of compassion. The other Gospel writers also convey this quality, of course, because it is so characteristic of Jesus. Matthew tells us several times that Jesus is "moved with compassion" as he looks at the multitudes. But it is Luke who makes this quality most real and most winsome, and he does so primar-

What are some examples of compassion in Luke's Gospel?

When have you experienced compassion—as a source? as a recipient? What makes it difficult to be compassionate in our time and culture? Do you think people were more compassionate in earlier times?

ily by the way he tells us of Jesus' activities and by his choice of parables.

So it is that Luke describes us as *lost*. This term in no way minimizes the fact of our sins; it simply approaches our condition from the posture of compassion. It is the word I would choose if I were talking with persons I loved deeply, if I wanted them to know the peril they were in, but at the same time to convey that I was hurting with them in their predicament.

I see this same quality of compassion in Luke's account of Jesus' synagogue sermon in Nazareth. Jesus tells his hometown audience that there were many widows in Israel in Elijah's time, yet Elijah was sent to a widow in the region of Sidon; and that there were many with leprosy in Israel in Elisha's time, but Elisha healed only Naaman the Syrian (4:25-27). This was a dramatic way of saying that God cares about the outsider. But it was also an offense to those who were not compassionate. So, too, with the parables in Luke 15, where the key word is *lost*; in showing compassion to the outsiders, Jesus offended those who saw themselves as having a favored status.

As for the parable of the good Samaritan, the word which would define the Samaritan best would surely be *compassionate*. There was no other reason to help the dying stranger. The Samaritan had no obligation to stop; it was patently foolhardy to do so. Compassion generally is somewhat foolhardy. It goes beyond the requirements of law, it burdens one's emotions, and it usually offers almost no prospect of return. *Compassion* is an involving kind of word, and it means getting involved when one is not required to do so. It is, in a sense, a human expression of grace.

In the story of the rich man and Lazarus (16:19-31), it is the absence of compassion that marks the character of the rich man. Cold logic can argue that the rich man owed Lazarus nothing; but of course the issue in compassion is that it is extended without debt or deserving. It is clear, from the way Jesus told the story, that the rich man was conscious of Lazarus's existence and even knew his name. But he did not

Choose two or three of the instances of Jesus' compassion mentioned in this section for discussion (such as the rich man and Lazarus, Luke 16:19-31). What does Jesus do? What is he asked, if anything? What happens? What does the experience teach us?

What is the difference between compassion and sentimentality?

involve himself in Lazarus's pain. He lacked compassion.

This mood of compassion seems to be a minor theme running through so many of Luke's stories. It is present in the raising of the widow's son at Nain (7:11-17); the widow makes no appeal (her son was dead; any appeal was useless), Jesus is touched by her heartbreak, and he asks her not to cry. When the sinful woman anoints Jesus at the home of Simon the Pharisee, Jesus expresses no discomfort, though the display had to be embarrassing; he responds with what can only be called compassion (7:36-50). And of course *compassion* is the operative word in Jesus' encounter with Zaccheus (19:1-10) and with the repentant thief (23:39-43). In each instance Jesus is daring to engage himself with the pain of some other person. This is the quality of compassion.

Contemporary observers say that many in the Western world—especially in the great urban centers—are suffering from "compassion fatigue," that is, they see so much pain and receive so many appeals for help that they simply run out of compassion. I expect that these observers are correct in their analysis. We are badly in need of the Jesus whom Luke describes.

The Impatience of Jesus

But Luke gives us an incongruity in his portrayal of Jesus. With all of our Lord's concern for the poor; with all of his attention to the outcast; and with his readiness to give time, unsolicited, to the needy; Jesus seems so often to be in a hurry. He brooks no nonsense from religious leaders. When his hometown people assume (typical of their time) that God favored the Jews above all others, Jesus challenges their smugness with his reference to Gentiles to whom God sent mercy. In the stories of the rich man and Lazarus and of the rich

What is your emotional response to what our author calls the impatience of Jesus during the period of Jesus' journey to Jerusalem?

Look over the story of the rich fool (Luke 12:13-21). Do you see any impatience in Jesus? What in the parable are we to observe about human smugness?

What is the place of repentance and forgiveness (Luke 6:24-25; 5:32)? Think quietly about the things for which you need to repent, those persons whom you need to forgive, and those from whom you need to seek forgiveness.

fool (12:13-21), Jesus has a reformer's impatience with those who feel secure in their wealth. When Luke records some of the beatitudes, such as "Blessed are the poor," he goes on to warn the rich that they are comfortable now, but that they will be hungry later (6:24-25).

But this care for the outcasts is also tough-minded; it never condones sin. Both Luke and Matthew tell how Jesus has come to call the sinners, not the righteous—like a doctor who tends to those who are sick. They go on to say that the sinners should repent and turn from their sins (5:32; Matthew 9:12-13). As Luke perceives it, Jesus' love for sinners is not so shortsighted as to leave them in their sins. He has come to heal, not to sympathize.

Luke's picture is not inconsistent. The same love that showed itself in compassion chose, in other instances, to thrust ahead with impatience. It was love that compelled Jesus to be done with religious nonsense and self-seeking. To use the language of a physician, it is as if Jesus looked out on a waiting room filled with desperately ill people and ordered the dilettantes to go home so that he might give his time to those who really needed him. Because time and energy are limited, love may become impatient with that which prevents love from doing its work.

Such, in brief, is Luke's portrait of Jesus Christ. It is the biography that an evangelist would write. It is not simply a compilation of data about Jesus, but the report of a person who has, quite gladly, been conquered by him.

5

LUKE CLARIFIES OUR VISION

If Luke were alive today, would he be viewed as a primitive rube whose ideas are embarrassingly outdated? Or would he perhaps shed new light on our understanding of our times? Is it possible that his perspective, nineteen centuries removed, could help him to see the forest of our times, where we have become specialists in twigs and leaves?

That is, do not all of our contemporary analysts suffer from nearsightedness? It would seem almost impossible for any native of our times to stand off and view them objectively; after all, we are part of both the problems and the possibilities, so we are inclined either to respond or to react. Whatever we observe about Luke's insights for our times reflects something of what we perceive our times to be. Short of pure objectivity, we must do the best we can to see ourselves as we are and to see how Luke might help us understand our times. It is an exercise worth doing—and doing prayerfully.

Our Contemporary Caesar

As we noted earlier, Luke wrote his Gospel for a culture that was dominated by the emperor. The emperors enjoyed being heralded as gods and were restive when anyone—like a Galilean street preacher—competed with them. So who is the emperor in our day? Obviously, no royal figure stands out. Indeed, just now we do not have even a collection of leaders such as the world knew in the days of Churchill, Stalin, Roosevelt, Hitler, Mussolini, and Hirohito. Nor does one country dominate the scene; rather, there is an uneasy jockeying between the European coalition, the

It is obviously impossible for any of us to view ourselves or our times with complete objectivity. How can we at least approach that goal? How can we be sensitive to our own prejudices?

United States, Japan, and China, with several other Asian and Middle East countries waiting to assert themselves.

But we have an emperor, one that in some ways is more powerful than history has ever known. I speak of the conglomerate of news, learning, entertainment, and sensation that we call the media. Their range of influence includes print, radio, movies, television, and now the extensive world of computer communication. They are not a monolith, but they are probably closer to it than we dare think. It is not because the various elements are bound together in a conspiracy of any sort, but because they tend to be driven by the same secular and materialistic impulses.

We can rightly say that never before in human history have the minds of so many been accessible to the influence of so few. The media is a power far more pervasive and infinitely more intrusive than any government that has ever existed. And because it is a power that seems to depend on a kind of democracy—that is, on the willingness of people to buy its product—we hardly realize how great its control can be.

So what would Luke say? I think he would treat this new emperor Media as he did Caesar. Luke used Caesar's highways to travel with the Gospel, accepted Caesar's peace, and constantly challenged Caesar's power when that power threatened to be ultimate. And especially, Luke would remind us of the power that is available to us, the power of the Holy Spirit. Luke's Gospel is rightly described as the Gospel of the Holy Spirit. When the angel appears to Mary, it is with the promise that "the Holy Spirit will come upon you" (Luke 1:35). When Mary and Elizabeth meet soon thereafter, Elizabeth is "filled with the Holy Spirit" (1:41). After John is born, Zechariah's tongue is loosed and he is "filled with the Holy Spirit" (1:67). And when

What contemporary world leaders stand out? Do any have the stature of a Churchill, a Roosevelt, or (negatively) a Hitler? Are leaders developed only in dramatically difficult times?

Studies indicate that media persons are generally not representative of the population as a whole. To what degree do you feel that the news is slanted by these factors? How can we choose our reading and listening so that we get a somewhat balanced view?

If the Holy Spirit is such an issue in our world, why don't we give a greater role to the Spirit? (See Luke 1:41; 2:25-27.)

LUKE'S MESSAGE

Jesus is brought to the Temple for rites of dedication, Simeon, a man on whom the Holy Spirit rests, is there to bless him (2:25-27).

I realize that what I have just said sounds very simplistic. For sheer data, it is simple. If one believes, as Luke did, that the Spirit of God has a stake in our world and its events, and if one believes that the Spirit of God is omnipresent, as Luke and the Scriptures maintain, it is quite right to say that we are better equipped than the media Caesar. But of course crucial issues remain: our readiness to trust the Spirit, our faith that God's Spirit is indeed able, and our maturity in working with God to the fulfilling of the divine will. So although my answer, through Luke, is simple, it is not simplistic.

Our Believing World

Ours is a believing world; it might even be said to be gullible. In much of the world the spiritual is getting more emphasis than it has in the recent past. The largest bookstores in the United States often label a section simply "Spiritual Issues," and include in it Judaism, Christianity, New Age, astrology, and perhaps some Eastern religions. One gets the feeling that the browsers see little difference between these several thought systems; they ask for neither spiritual nor intellectual discrimination.

And perhaps it is not stretching a point to say that the same readiness to believe exists in those countries of the Western world where large percentages of people claim to be entirely separated from religion, even to the point of identifying themselves as atheists. Almost always such persons find a substitute for religion, perhaps particularly in their opposition to organized religion.

The late Paul Tillich defined religion as that which is our ultimate concern. It is a rare individual who does not have some ultimate concern. Many would not be able to define their concern, but this uncertainty only adds to the pathos.

Would you describe our world as gullible? What evidence do you see, in reading or conversations, that might support this view? If not gullible, how would you describe it?

Someone has said that we humans are "believing animals"—that is, that we insist on having something in which to believe. Do you think this is true? Why?

How could our world get a more appealing picture of Jesus?

The human spirit, like nature, abhors a vacuum. We want something in which to believe, something that impels us. Our generation is hard on the quest for such a grand impulse. We are the believing generation.

Luke wrote his Gospel for just such a world. As we indicated earlier, Paul identified the people of Athens as "extremely religious" (Acts 17:22), with gods of every kind. Their bookstores, so to speak, would look very much like ours, except that Christianity was just beginning to get a reading. Luke, following his mentor, Paul, would thrust himself boldly into such a culture. He would be confident that Jesus Christ can be presented to a believing world without apology. He surely would not retreat from the field.

But what would he say to such a world? Luke does not offer much of a structured theology in his Gospel. Rather, he presents Jesus as he knows him. This is partly a matter of Jesus' teaching and more especially of his deeds. When Paul preached to the "extremely religious" at Athens,

he introduced them to the Resurrection, the answer to humanity's most penetrating question. I venture Luke would do the same. After all, he ends his biography with the believers so captured by Jesus' resurrection and ascension that they are "continually in the temple blessing God" (Luke 24:53).

Lost in the Crowd

Luke might be amazed at the masses of people in our modern cities; his was a world of agriculture and tradespeople. But the farms were generally small and (except for the nomads) the people lived very close together in the cities. Large yards are a modern luxury. The streets were narrow, and much business was carried on in the out-of-doors; so daily life in Jerusalem, Athens, or Alexandria might have seemed almost as hectic as in a modern city.

Nevertheless, people did not live on top of one another in the fashion of our modern, massive apartment complexes. And

---

List some of the factors that make our world impersonal.

Nothing is so radical (that is, so much at the root of the matter) as to truly believe in the worth of individuals. Who seems to you to demonstrate this quality in our day?

Review again Luke 15:3-32 with an eye for the individual. How are they regarded? treated? What does this mean for us as individuals?

Lost sheep; lost coin;

because people were not isolated from one another in automobiles or in heated and air-conditioned dwellings, they knew one another. Luke would notice that we have so many people and—comparatively—so few friends. He would probably be appalled at the impersonal quality of our lives. He might wonder if it is possible to remain fully human when so many of our relationships are so superficial, so hurried, and thus—in the largest metropolitan areas—so often on the edge of irritation and anger.

We live in a lonely crowd. With the urban turning into the megalopolis, with cities of five million and more a commonplace on every continent except Antarctica, and with predictions that in time the east coast of America will be one continuous city from Boston (or perhaps even Bangor) to Miami, and the west coast a city from Seattle to Mexico, we cannot help asking ourselves, "Who matters in a world as big and as crowded as this? Do I matter at all?" It is a very lonely feeling.

Luke speaks directly to this need. No one is more radical than he in his insistence on the value of the individual. Where John declares, rightly, that God so loved the world, Luke speaks of a single coin, a single sheep, a single son—and declares that all of heaven celebrates the finding of just one lost individual (15:3-32). If God has such ultimate concern for an individual (any individual), we are persons of ultimate worth. We matter profoundly. Again and again, as we read Luke's Gospel, we get the feeling that Jesus saw only individuals. He was not taken with movements, systems, or agendas, but with some single, lost person.

Women in the World

The world has been made up of two sexes from the very beginning; "male and female [God] created them" (Genesis 1:27). But until relatively recently, at most times and in most places of the world, the two sexes were not seen as equal. Now a great ferment engages our society. It is a ferment that, I suspect, will never be fully settled; there will always be an uneasy shifting of boundaries, especially in a rapidly changing world. And of course there will always be quite differ-

Review the Scriptures mentioned in "Women in the World." List some evidences and instances of Luke's concern for women. Do you see any pattern in his approach?

How would Luke help men understand women? How would he help women appreciate themselves more?

ent opinions as to where those boundaries should lie. But I doubt that ever again the world will be content to think that one sex should be seen as inherently inferior to the other.

Would Luke, living in a world so removed from ours, have anything to say to this changing scene? Could he contribute any order to a flux that promises to engage us for generations to come?

Luke is no social engineer. He offered no psychological theories about the nature of the sexes. But it is fascinating to see how many of those who study Luke's Gospel come to refer to it as "the Gospel of Women." As we indicated earlier, it is Luke who dates events in the unfolding of his plot, not by the political calendar but by the ancient and intimate calendar of a woman's pregnancy (Luke 1:26). Luke unfolds his story around Elizabeth and Mary, with Zechariah providing an introduction. Luke tells us about Anna (2:36-38) and includes the gentle insights of a mother's concern for a lost son (2:48) and her maternal memory bank (2:51).

It is Luke who includes the story of the raising of the widow of Nain's son, and who does so with the simple pathos of, "He was his mother's only son, and she was a widow" (7:12). Luke

> **Luke sees women with quality and intends us to know that Jesus viewed them that way.**

not only tells us the story of the woman "who was a sinner" who anointed Jesus' feet with her tears, but he very clearly makes the woman the heroine of the story, and the man Simon the villain (7:36-50).Twice Luke makes women the key figures in parables (15:8-10; 18:1-8). And when Luke tells us of the women who aided in the ministry of Jesus, he gives us additional details about some of these women (8:1-3). In doing so he pays them the high tribute of identifying them as individuals. No doubt about it, Luke sees women with quality and intends us to know that Jesus viewed them that way.

Would Luke add measurably to our understanding and to our ability to deal effectively with this significant issue of women in a changing world? It would be presumptuous and intellectually dishonest to project specific data from these generalized indications of Luke's attitude. But I think it is not unfair to say that all social reform depends at least on the attitudes that we bring to our circumstances and problems. So often our greatest problem is not to find solutions, but to have the will to deal with the problems and to deal with them intelligently, sympathetically, and fairly.

I do not think Luke would

intend to give us a specific agenda for the female/male issues we face. But he would want us to see the worth of people in general and of women in particular. And this is by no means simply a matter of men gaining a more perceptive understanding of women; it is also a matter of women coming to appreciate themselves. Luke would help with this.

A Sick World

Ours is a sick world. Patterns of conduct that other generations described as sin are today classified as sickness. Alcoholism is the most notable example. Gambling, too, is in this category. When someone commits a quite horrendous crime, the reaction is almost always, "A person would have to be sick to do a thing like that."

This specialized use of the language of sickness no doubt reflects our contemporary emphasis on sociology, psychiatry, and psychology as well as recent scientific discoveries that bring insight to pathological origins of certain illnesses. Each generation makes its particular contribution to human understanding. One unique emphasis of this century has been to compile mountainous case studies and statistical research that helps us identify and define the parameters of healthy human behavior and explain the origins of unhealthy or dysfunctional behaviors, beliefs, and attitudes. In so doing, we tend to avoid the use of terms that are considered to be morally judgmental. Thus many contemporary scholars avoid using a word like *sin*, partly because they see it as a term of opprobrium. Many consider sin outside the realm of scientific definition, although the late, prominent psychiatrist Karl Menninger insisted that sin is both a valid and a necessary concept.

Nevertheless, popular usage has narrowed the definition of *sin* almost to a point of removing it from much public discourse, while greatly enlarging the meaning of *sickness*. Some observers suggest that in time all human conduct will be explained, at least in the minds of many, as a result of forces beyond personal control—glands, genetic codes, environment.

No one among the biblical writers would enter this discussion more easily than Luke. As we have indicated earlier, Luke had

Is it possible to use the term *sin* without being judgmental?

Compare *lostness* and *sickness* to *sin*. What unique qualities does each word bring to your insight?

his own special understanding of our human condition; he saw us as lost. This term, as we said before, does not seem as harsh as "sinner"; but the condition it describes is ultimately just as destructive.

As a physician, Luke would probably be empathetic with the idea of using *sickness* as a synonym for *sin*. "Salvation," after all, has the same root word as "salve" and in its classical form always carries something of the idea of healing. Sin is indeed the sickness of the soul, and Luke would probably not be averse to seeing himself as a physician of the soul as well as a physician of the body.

Luke might be amused at the way some in our time are uncomfortable with the concept of sin, but he probably would not allow himself to be bogged down in issues of language. If I understand Luke's attitude rightly, he would be more interested in the patient's welfare than in the spelling of the prescription.

The Atomization of Society

A strange thing has happened while our generation was on its way to unity and understanding. Our differences have become more numerous than ever.

The twentieth century was to have been the century of world peace. Improved means of communication seemed to mean that nations would understand one another better, and that messages could be received with a minimum of delay. Students began to travel more freely from one country to another, offering still more opportunities for better international understanding. But even with such positive foundations for peace, the twentieth century has endured two World Wars and a continuing series of regional conflicts, even to this very moment. And the explosion of knowledge has included, tragically, the development of weapons that can wipe out the human race.

Early in this century, the United States was still recovering from its

---

What differences do you see in race relations in your particular country or community, as you compare the present with a decade or two ago? What differences in the role of women?

Most of us will acknowledge that wealth is unevenly distributed in our world. What can any of us do about this concern? Is it so complex as to be completely out of our control?

As you think of the persons you know, what varieties of taste do you see in reading matter, music, art, and humor?

several centuries of slavery and the war (1861–65) that had brought an end to that practice. At the same time, women were working for the kind of equality that would grant them the right to vote. Much progress has been made in both these areas. The descendants of slaves in America are now coming more and more to be part of the nation's economic middle class; and women not only vote, but are gradually being recognized for their potential leadership in politics, business, and the professions. But with all of that, any sensitive observer realizes that the gains thus far achieved are still very tenuous and that they are by no means widespread. Still worse, in some instances those very gains are resented by others, so that the steps of progress are not always met with thanksgiving.

The door of opportunity in the United States opened vastly wider following World War II, as university and professional education became available to literally millions of new persons. The spread of the educational structure has eventually made it possible for virtually everyone in America to receive either a college or a trade school education. As a result,

In most instances a relative few have gained substantially while great masses of people are still living at a far lower economic standard.

economic security ought presumably to be in reach for a much larger share of the population.

These and other gains would seem to guarantee a much more unified human race, both in the United States and in the world. With so many educational, cultural, racial, and ethnic barriers removed, the possibilities of mutual understanding and sympathy are, potentially, much more hopeful.

But at the same time, other changes have complicated our human scene. Increased wealth in both the Western nations and in the developing nations has not been evenly distributed; to the contrary, in most instances a relative few have gained substantially while great masses of people are still living at a far lower economic standard. And while great efforts have been made to bring world unity, ancient ethnic and tribal divisions have reasserted themselves in Africa, central Europe, and many parts of Asia. In the United States and in some other parts of the Western world, strident new differences have appeared. Where once there was rather general agreement in matters of music, humor, and entertainment, today the younger and the older (as well as some other societal differences) have dramatically different preferences in all these matters. Magazine stands that once carried a relatively limited number of general interest publications are now the setting for a vast variety of specialized publications of almost every imaginable kind. In matters of taste and culture, Western society is diverse to a point that is sometimes almost antagonistic.

Luke would offer no panacea. I think he would simply proceed in his customary fashion of seeing all the human race as beloved of God and therefore deserving of his loving concern. The spirit that made Luke embrace "the least, the last, and the lost," and that brought forth his special sympathy for women, for social outsiders, and for the poor, would reach out inclusively to the stunningly diverse elements in our late-twentieth-century culture.

Would this solve our problems? We cannot say. But I am very sure that it is a witness we need and that Luke would urge us—passionately—to provide.

Would Luke understand our times, different as they seem from his? I believe he would. I believe it partly because I think that sensitive human beings in any generation and any culture are quick to discern the realities beneath the apparent. And I believe it because I believe that Luke was especially sensitive to God's Holy Spirit, the Spirit that is quite free of time constraints.

6

LUKE LOOKS AT THE THIRD MILLENNIUM

Who would dare to predict what the next millennium will be like? In truth, almost anyone and everyone. Very few subjects are so popular just now, both in the media and in general conversation, as predictions of what we can anticipate in the third millennium.

Of course everyone knows that such predicting is risky business. It always has been. Irving Fischer, a noted economics professor at Yale University in the 1920's, predicted in early 1929 that stocks had reached what looked like "a permanently high plateau." Ponder that prediction when you look at the current Dow Jones average!

In 1943, Thomas Watson, the chair of IBM and at the time probably the most knowledgeable person in the world in matters of office procedures, said, "I think there is a world market for maybe five computers." *Popular Mechanics* has always been venturesome and forward-looking. It concluded in 1949 that "computers in the future may weigh no more than one and a half tons." Think about that when you tuck your laptop under your arm this evening.

If predictions were risky in 1929 and 1949, they are practically surrealistic today. Nevertheless, we cannot help wondering about this millennium that is now so near at hand. Still more, we cannot help asking ourselves how we will cope with it.

Our wondering is not to be discredited. Rather, it should be treated with respect. After all,

What is it that so captivates us about a new millennium? Why should the year 2000 or 2001 be any more significant than 1998 or 1999?

Look over some past, apparently absurd, predictions. What others come to mind? Have you made some conversational predictions at some time that you hope your friends have forgotten?

unless Christ returns or history turns some cataclysmic corner, we will very soon be inhabitants of the third millennium. We ought therefore to put forth an intelligent effort to estimate what it will be like and how we should live in it. And true to our theme, we will seek Luke's counsel; that is, the counsel Luke gives us via his record of the life and teachings of Jesus Christ.

An Era of Rapid Change

Of course it would be altogether foolhardy to predict many specific details about the coming millennium. Space, if not wisdom, will restrain me. It can be safely said, in any event, that we will live more than ever in a world of rapid change. Some of this change will come from the seemingly endless round of discoveries in the world of mechanics, electronics, science, and physics. No doubt even greater changes in these fields are on the horizon.

Changes will also come because of our human restlessness. At some point in the nineteenth century, we humans opened some sort of Pandora's box. I doubt that we will ever again be content with things as they are. Progress is insatiable; if change is not gain, some are satisfied to get change for change's sake.

Others are much more resistant, because change challenges the status quo, the familiar, the comfortable. The time matters not; fear of and discomfort with change is itself perennial. John the Baptist came with a new message of repentance—change of heart, mind, and behavior—and he literally lost his head in the endeavor (Luke 3:1-20; Mark 6:14-29).

Jesus, of course, ushered in an

What changes in travel and communication can you envision for the next decade? In what ways will these changes improve the quality of life? How might they diminish it?

Are we now so committed to the very principle of change that we will change whether or not change represents true progress?

People often talk about being "on the cutting edge." Has that philosophy become an end in itself? Are our trends sometimes turning in on themselves?

What changes did John the Baptist and Jesus demand in their ministries? Review Luke 3:1-15 and 4:16-22, 29-30. What does their call mean for us today?

era of revolutionary change, although the length and depth to which that change extends is still unfathomable. His early hearers knew that something was afoot from his "first day in church," when he both astonished and angered the gathered listeners (Luke 4:14-30). The world continues to reject and embrace, to dread and anticipate the new age and new life in Jesus Christ. Regardless of our affections and antipathies, change will occur.

But although we can be sure that the new millennium will be a period of continuing and probably even accelerating change, we cannot say what it will be. We can observe the trends, of course, but we can only say with certainty that trends change. After all, even a return to "the good old days," impossible as that is, would be a change.

Urbanization

It seems almost inevitable that our world will become still more urbanized in the third millennium. Although it is likely that efforts will be made to limit the number of births, it is unlikely that the world will get to a place of zero population growth.

Cultural bias toward male children, poverty, war, and hunger are mighty influences on the decision to have, to keep, and to raise children. On another side, continued improvements in nutrition and health care will extend life for those fortunate enough to have access to it. This will "crowd" the planet still more.

While we may think that only some unimaginable disaster or plague or a massive war would be likely to reduce the earth's population, we are confronted with the chilling reality of the spread of AIDS worldwide and its debilitating effects on the population. Wars in Africa and Eastern Europe, for example, have, with AIDS, created a vast army of orphans, surely the most vulnerable citizens in the world. Their crowding into urban centers, along with all the other factors that draw persons to the city, will continue to make survival in urban settings tenuous.

Urbanization seems to carry with it some deleterious changes in human character. The traits that make life more livable—trust, courtesy, thoughtfulness, personal worth, a sense of belonging— seem so often to be victims of urbanization. Will life in the next millennium be longer, but less liv-

What urbanization have you experienced in the past ten years? How has it affected your lifestyle? What are the gains? What are the losses? Have any of these changes affected your spiritual life?

able? Is the quality of life doomed to deterioration in the next millennium? Perhaps not. The unquenchable human spirit is in many places rising above the fray as urban residents are fighting in healthy and effective ways to reclaim the safety of their homes.

Global Community

National boundaries may remain as significant as ever in the new millennium, but the inhabitants of each country will be increasingly diverse. Speed of transportation and communication is making it easier for people to take up residence in another country without losing touch with their own culture or families.

Where once corporations moved their employees from one city or state or province to another, now they are as likely to move them halfway around the world. As these corporations come increasingly to be owned by persons in scores of countries, such movement can only increase. Furthermore, as multinational ownership of corporations increases, the impetus to international activity will accelerate still more.

America has always claimed the title of "melting pot," but the validity of that image is undergoing rightful challenge. The United States population includes a mix now that would have been unimaginable in earlier generations, as Hispanic, Asian, and Middle Eastern peoples swell the ranks of new immigrants. These new citizens and residents are bringing to American eyes the vision of retaining native culture while participating in the society around them. We are more than ever a salad of distinct and unique flavors rather than a melted together blend of one taste.

This phenomenon is not unique

How many dwellings have you lived in during the past twenty years? In how many cities, states, provinces, or countries?

Do you now have in your neighborhood or church a person from another country? Have you or a member of your family traveled in another continent? Has it been an area where you have felt strange or out of place spiritually or in which you welcomed the diversity?

Is there a house of worship for an Eastern religion anywhere in your area? How does your congregation feel about it? Why?

What effects, if any, are you experiencing as our country blends and changes in terms of its ethnicity?

to the US. Vast areas of England's cities are now Asian, especially Indian; France has a substantial African population; and Germany's immigrant workers from Africa and the Middle East have at times dramatically affected its social and economic scene.

These changes have of course affected the religious landscape. The religion pages of American newspapers in most larger cities now carry news of Buddhist and Islamic communities. One wonders how long it will be before a representative of one of the Eastern religions offers a ceremonial prayer at a national political convention or for the inauguration of a president or a governor.

Issues of religious persecution, in those countries where the dominant religious body has active militant adherents, will become a more serious international concern. So while national boundaries will remain, individual nations may come to seem like tribes within a world nation.

But an especially fascinating issue of boundaries will come in the millennium. As a child, I waited each Sunday for a comic strip that fantasized about *Buck Rogers in the 25th Century*. Then the idea of exploring outer space was indeed fantasy, and the twenty-fifth-century setting was simply a way of saying that it was

Inner space is also a frontier ripe for exploration.

remote beyond imagining. But now it is, if not an immediate issue, at least an imaginable one. Will our next frontier be outer space? If so, how will this affect not simply our politics and economics but also our perception of our own human worth?

When one moves into a new and unfamiliar environment, one often suffers a crisis of identity. Will our world as a whole suffer some such crisis as the boundaries of our potential environment stretch beyond all previous definitions? For some time it has been popular to speak of persons needing to find out "who they are"; that issue may take on vast new dimensions in the new millennium—and if it does, the psychiatric and counseling professions will be challenged to the limit. Inner space is also a frontier ripe for exploration.

Secular and Spiritual

An ancient generation sought to build a tower to heaven (Genesis 11:1-9). The third millennium may see its own version of the Babel tower. The future threatens, on the one hand, to be unabashedly secular. Every circumstance will encourage it. The burgeoning growth of knowledge, especially in areas of electronic discovery, will make humans think we are the masters of our fate. Medical discoveries will heighten this feeling; the ability to clone and perhaps even to take hold of the thunderbolt of life will bring a new birth of arrogance. Such hubris is essentially a declaration of independence from God.

But we humans will not allow a spiritual void. The third millennium is likely to see an uneasy alliance between the secular and the spiritual. The spiritual that will lay its claim on the new millennium will be a tenuous one, however. It may offer religion without commitment and benefits without sacrifice. A secular age will demand a religion, but it may tend to the magic: a religion that guarantees favors without insisting on character. This is nothing new, of course; it was the essence of ancient Baal worship. But it will have new accoutrements and new glamour in the third millennium. It may well present Christianity's greatest challenge since the Enlightenment.

Can Luke Help Us?

Nearly a third of a century ago Joseph Wood Krutch, probably one of the most respected social observers of the mid-twentieth century, tried to peer into the third millennium. Along the way, Krutch observed that most of the prophets are inclined, "for the most part," to "take no account of those intangibles—mental, moral, or emotional —which some are probably quite apt to dismiss as mere by-products of economic and social conditions" (*Saturday Review*, January 20, 1968, page 14).

Krutch went on to say, "Nevertheless, the quality of life in the year 2000 may depend as much upon such beliefs, attitudes, and faiths as it does upon the trends recognized by most of the prophets." His words need to be spoken loudly to the brave new world of the third millennium. This millennium will not only need a sustaining faith, it will need it more desperately than its predecessors—precisely because the stakes are larger and the perils greater.

What exactly makes for "quality of life," in either the first century or the twenty-first? It is not bread alone, as Jesus told the tempter in

What do you think the author means by the phrase, "an uneasy alliance between the secular and the spiritual"? Does the secular destroy the spiritual, or simply pervert it? Explain.

Try to recast the John Wood Krutch insight in your own language, as you see life unfolding on the edge of the third millennium. What does this mean to you?

the wilderness (Luke 4:4). Nor will our needs be satisfied with a wondrous, unceasing excitement of discoveries and "progress." Augustine—a notable intellect and sensualist in his own right—knew whereof he spoke when he declared that God has made us for himself, and that our hearts are restless until they find their rest in God.

A new millennium will discover that its answers are only new questions, and that its distractions cannot ultimately silence the incessant cry for reality. It is just possible that the new millennium will compel us to realize that we are more (as some essayist has said) than trousered apes. Our abundance will itself prove disgusting. We will demand food worthy of creatures made in the image of God.

In such a quest, the third millennium will not settle for mere religiosity. Luke tells us of the prayers of a Pharisee and a publican. The difference between the two is clear and dramatic. The Pharisee desires a religion that will allow him to be satisfied with himself; the publican confesses a desperate need for the reality of acceptance by God. The Pharisee believes he deserves God's favor, and he congratulates himself on that fact. The publican—who is actually a far more religious person than the Pharisee—knows that he needs more than superficial religion can give.

The pendulum of religion seems to swing back and forth from one period to another, so any predictions are perilous; nor will any prediction be true everywhere at the same time, except in some period of extraordinary revival. Nevertheless, I dare to feel that the third millennium will insist on religion with reality, or not at all. Surfeited with excitement and sensualism, weary of its own remarkable devices, and embarrassed by the failure of its best wisdom, the new millennium will ask for reality. Its posture will be closer to that of the publican than that of the Pharisee. Our abundance will convince us of our poverty.

"Our abundance will itself prove disgusting." What does this have to do with some of our excesses as you have observed them? Whose abundance does this refer to? How might we take care of those who have a deficit of income, food, health, or dignity?

"The new millennium will ask for reality." Do some eras find satisfaction enough in the superficial? Are generations different in the depth or intensity of their spiritual quest? Explain.

It will be an era especially sensitive to Luke's call to the lost. Like the prodigal, it is wasting its resources in irresponsible living. Like the coin and the sheep, it is somehow pathetic in its helplessness and lostness. But if it is to be restored, it will need to follow the ancient path of being sorry for its sins and turning from them (15:7, 10). Because while Luke describes their condition as lost, when they are found they identify themselves as those who have sinned.

And What of the City?

Luke would acknowledge that the city will present a problem in the new millennium. He saw it as a point of divine sorrow even in the first century. Twice in Luke's account, Jesus looks at Jerusalem and expresses his sorrow (13:31-35; 19:41-44). For the Jews, Jerusalem was the major city, the truly special city. More than Athens, Rome, or Alexandria, it was Jerusalem that symbolized all that a city was supposed to be.

Thus when Jesus wept at Jerusalem's spiritual stupor, the significance was profound. If even Jerusalem could go wrong, then what hope could there be for the other cities that were by nature secular and irreligious?

I think Jesus would call his followers to weep for the cities and to embrace them as he sought to embrace Jerusalem. Without a doubt, cities are more difficult to win to the will of God than are villages and the countryside. Because of their impersonal nature, evil is pursued with less restraint. Historian Frederick Jackson Turner's study of the frontier revealed that moral disorders increase on the frontier because people are far removed from those who know them or their family. Cities now constitute a kind of permanent frontier. Conduct that would be unthinkable in a smaller community is accepted in a city because of the basic anonymity in a vast population. The only thing that can save cities from themselves is a grand moral change in their inhabitants.

Review Luke 13:31-35 and 19:41-44. Does this lament ring true for any cities of our era? Which ones? Why? What is the answer to the lament?

Urban areas are not the only candidates for sorrow. Is there really a difference in community and "moral fiber" in less urban areas? In what ways are suburban and rural areas needful of ministry?

What are the spaces in which we get lost? are lost? What can the community of faith do to find the lost?

In the second instance of our Lord's weeping for Jerusalem, Luke tells specifically of the coming destruction of Jerusalem. Jesus' lament has unique significance, of course; and yet in a sense what he said for Jerusalem could be said for any city—that their judgment has come because they did not recognize the time of God's visitation (19:44). The church's magnificent task in the third millennium will be to present God's heart with such clarity that the vast urban complexes of the world will hear and respond.

The church's magnificent task in the third millennium will be to present God's heart with clarity.

Lost in Space

But what shall we say of the vast varieties of peoples, cultures, and religious commitments that will characterize not only the cities, but the entire population of the third millennium? Suppose, even, that the next millennium reveals inhabitants on another planet that we would classify as human; how would Luke have us understand such a possibility?

I think Luke's answer would be quite uncomplicated. He would say, "Are they lost? If so, the Savior is for them." Luke had a wonderful capacity for reducing our human condition to basic fundamentals. He was able to look past Jew and Samaritan, haves and have-nots, men and women, Pharisee and publican, to the point of our root humanity. He would see us at the focus of our need. And because we are human, our need—above and beyond all—is God.

We humans are obviously so different in so many ways. Consider the difference in subsistence income in an African village and an American suburb; or for that matter, the difference in gross income between an American laborer and an American mega-executive. Or the difference between the person who lives in illiteracy, and the one who reads and writes in several languages, or whose ultimate pleasure is in the delicate nuances of eloquence. Or the cultural preferences that range from Rembrandt to number painting, and from Beethoven to rap. Is there any common denominator? Just this, that we are all of us made in God's image, and that each of us, in some fashion, hungers for God and shows our unique and complementary createdness through the gifts and appreciation that we have been given.

Luke found a bond of human need in the Samaritan and the Jew by the side of the road; he established a field of comparison (probably to Simon's discomfort) between Simon the Pharisee and the woman of poor reputation who intruded upon his dinner party. With a wonderful sense of breadth, Luke saw us humans as sisters and brothers indeed, all of us kin in our need of the Christ whom Luke adored.

The Need for Prayer

Luke's particular insights on prayer are significant to the third millennium. The parables of the man who, in midnight need, kept asking his neighbor's help until he got it, and the widow who pursued the unjust judge until he gave in to her unyielding pleading are parables with a common message. They offer an insight on prayer that is present at other places in the Scriptures, but never more clearly than in these two stories.

The Hebrew prophet, Daniel, tells of a prayer experience where he prayed for an extended period, and got his answer only because he held on (Daniel 10:2-14). Paul describes one aspect of prayer as a struggling with evil (Ephesians 6:12). Certainly Jesus' own prayer in Gethsemane is of this quality (Luke 22:39-44).

But nowhere, I repeat, is the point more sharply defined than in the two parables on prayer that only Luke gives us (11:5-8; 18:1-8). We can rightly describe them as prayers for desperate circumstances. As I indicated earlier, Jesus told the two stories with wonderful touches of humor, but perhaps the humor was present precisely because of the poignancy of the subject. What do you do when your need is great and the time is short? If, that is, your unexpected guest has arrived and you have only minutes to meet his need, or someone is taking unfair advantage, and you know that before long you will be destroyed? What then? And what, particularly, if your requests seem to be rebuffed?

Luke reports that Jesus said that we "need to pray always and not to lose heart" (18:1). I cannot imagine a more significant word for the third millennium. Optimistic as I am, I nevertheless sense that the new millennium will present titanic issues. How

Prayer is experienced in many ways; Jesus said that God knows what we need before we ask. Why, then, did Jesus emphasize in Luke's parables the idea of insistence in prayer?

Review Luke 11:9-10 and 18:1. What does it mean to ask, seek, and knock? to never give up praying? Does this advice have effect in concrete situations or it is a theory about prayer? Explain.

can we possibly meet them? I venture that at times in the new millennium believers will feel forsaken, with their prayers apparently fruitless. How shall we respond? We must follow Luke's counsel from Jesus: we will keep knocking, keep insisting, never giving up (11:9-10). We will proceed in the rugged confidence that God is with us in our passion for a world hurt sore.

Over the centuries, the emphasis on prayer has ebbed and flowed in the church. The most impassioned prayer has usually come at times of human disaster—war, plagues, poverty. The best praying has always come from those persons who saw the importance of communion with God and particularly of prayer as an instrument for effecting the purposes of God. Perhaps in the third millennium there can be a rebirth of prayer, so that in crisis or not, the community of believers will realize that they are the strategic force for sanity in a culture that will often edge toward the abyss. Knowing this, they will pray in season and out of season.

The Close of the Age

Some will see this season as the last; the beginning of the end. The ancient Jews were warned to observe the signs of the times. John the Baptist sent a delegation to Jesus asking, "Are you the one?" Jesus announced with some drama the advent of the Kingdom, a cataclysmic event in which "one will be taken and the other left" (17:20-37). His ominous answer to where all this would take place: where "the vultures will gather" (17:37).

In spite of our amazing advances in science and technology, many see the vultures gathering in a world in which Christians take up arms against Christians; in which members of the clergy abuse their office by molesting innocents; in which hunger, disease, war, poverty, illiteracy, and horrible abuses against women and children are apparently commonplace.

Advances in communication not only allow us to watch a war in the comfort of our living rooms; they permit us to upload

Read Luke 17:20-37. What are the signs of the Kingdom? Do you see evidence of those signs now? If so, where?

Do you see places where "the vultures gather"? What is the responsibility of the community of faith to scatter the "vultures"?

What is the truth of the gospel for you? How has Luke's orderly account helped you to offer your own account?

and download the most profound and profane ideas in the ethereal world of "Netizens."

What words do we follow? Is this the time when we "will long to see one of the days of the Son of Man, and [we] will not see it" (17:22)? We do not know; but the signs of catastrophe, as well as of blessing, are obvious. The Gospels tell us plainly that only God knows which millennium will be the last. They also tell us, in "an orderly account," how to live our lives according to "the truth" (1:1, 4).

The Sum of It All

At the beginning of the first millennium of the Christian era, Luke had a story to tell. As we have already indicated, he was an evangelist-biographer.

Although he was obviously a scholar, Luke spoke with the insistence of an advocate. But he was not simply an advocate for Jesus Christ; he was also an advocate for the human race. He had diagnosed our needs, at least as they existed in his time; and he was obviously overjoyed to declare the remedy.

The world is more than ever obsessed with the material, possessed by demons of insatiable desire, desperately wanting human relationships but so often bumbling in our pursuit. We are transparently in need of a Savior. To this third millennium, Luke would say, "Here is the One who came to seek and to save those who are lost. Your millennium fits that description. I rejoice in presenting the Answer to your dilemma."

It is easy to see that Luke was an advocate for Jesus Christ, but how was he "an advocate for the human race"?